Colour Your Cortex

Bring your learning to life through the mindful art of colouring. Offering an alternative style of learning, this insightful book combines easy-to-follow explanations of brain anatomy and functions with detailed, labelled diagrams to colour in. While colouring, you can sit back, relax, and listen to the accompanying online audio podcast, which clearly explains each topic.

The unique interactive book covers a comprehensive list of brain anatomy, including how our brains grow, brain cells and how they communicate, important functions of the brain, brain disorders and reactions, and how our brains are protected. Using a conversational tone throughout, each chapter engages the reader with succinct descriptions of each topic, allowing them to easily digest and process the information, as they colour in the accompanying diagram. The book then concludes with a chapter on mindfulness and what benefits it can have for your brain and learning.

Designed to simplify complex concepts into bite-sized, understandable chunks, this is the ideal resource for psychology, neuroscience, nursing, and medical students who prefer visual and audible methods of learning. This book is also for anyone interested in understanding more about brain anatomy and functions, but with a little fun, creativity, and relaxation along the way.

Emma Randles is a private tutor from Wrexham who teaches in psychology and is about to start her PhD in cancer research at Wrexham University, associated with the Wrexham Maelor Academic Unit of Medical and Surgical Sciences. She has a first-class honours degree in Psychology with Neuropsychology and gained a distinction in her MSc in Biomedical Science. She recently won an award from Bangor University for her BSc research, which was neuropsychology-based. Being diagnosed with dyslexia has enabled her to find her own unique learning style, and she is passionate about helping students find their own learning techniques that suit their needs and allow them to excel.

Colour Your Cortex

A Visual and Audio Approach to the Study of the Brain

Emma Randles

Routledge
Taylor & Francis Group

LONDON AND NEW YORK

Cover Image: © Getty Images

First published 2024
by Routledge
4 Park Square, Milton Park, Abingdon, Oxon OX14 4RN

and by Routledge
605 Third Avenue, New York, NY 10158

Routledge is an imprint of the Taylor & Francis Group, an informa business

© 2024 Emma Randles

The right of Emma Randles to be identified as author of this work has been asserted in accordance with sections 77 and 78 of the Copyright, Designs and Patents Act 1988.

British Library Cataloguing-in-Publication Data
A catalogue record for this book is available from the British Library

Library of Congress Cataloging-in-Publication Data
Names: Randles, Emma, author.
Title: Colour your cortex : a visual and audio approach to the study of the brain / Emma Randles.
Description: Abingdon, Oxon ; New York, NY : Routledge, 2024. |
    Includes bibliographical references and index.
Identifiers: LCCN 2023047645 (print) | LCCN 2023047646 (ebook) |
    ISBN 9781032643205 (hardback) | ISBN 9781032643168 (paperback) |
    ISBN 9781032643236 (ebook)
Subjects: LCSH: Brain–Popular works. | Neurophysiology–Popular works. |
    Brain–Anatomy–Popular works. | Brain–Localization of functions–Popular works.
Classification: LCC QP376 .R358 2024 (print) | LCC QP376 (ebook) |
    DDC 612.8/2–dc23/eng/20240124
LC record available at https://lccn.loc.gov/2023047645
LC ebook record available at https://lccn.loc.gov/2023047646

ISBN: 978-1-032-64320-5 (hbk)
ISBN: 978-1-032-64316-8 (pbk)
ISBN: 978-1-032-64323-6 (ebk)

DOI: 10.4324/9781032643236

Designed and typeset in Scala Sans Pro by Alex Lazarou

Access the Audio Companion and Downloadable Content at:
www.routledge.com/9781032643168

Illustrations courtesy of Emma Randles, Luna, and Farhan

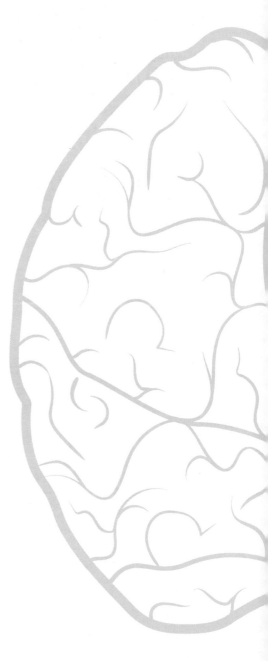

Contents

CONTENTS

Acknowledgements

Writing this book has been both a privilege and a challenge. I want to thank my friends for their continuous enthusiasm, interest, and motivation. To the family members who have supported me throughout my continuing academic journey and my book writing process – I will be forever grateful. I would also like to thank my tutors and lecturers from Bangor University and University of Salford for providing me with knowledge, encouragement, and a passion for learning. I am very thankful for the ongoing support from my MPhil/PhD supervisors, Dr Jixin Yang, Professor Stephen Hughes and Professor Iqbal Shergill at Wrexham University. Lastly, I would like to thank the reader for purchasing this book – I hope you find it useful.

In my experience, being a student with dyslexia is not easy – it requires patience, resilience, and the ability to find a learning style that works for you. I would like anybody who finds typical 'textbook learning' difficult to remember that you can do it and to never give up.

Emma Randles

Introduction

Studying can be hard – especially when it comes to memorising anatomy. Learning about the brain and its structures is vital for many subjects, such as psychology, neuroscience, medicine, psychiatry, and many more.

Sure, there are lots of things to learn about the brain. After all, our brains are capable of wonderful things, so it is no surprise that there are complex anatomical structures in the brain.

But ... learning all of this does not need to be stressful, tiresome, or boring.

Using this book, you can bring learning to life, through the mindful art of colouring. While relaxing, you can become familiar with anatomical names and the location of brain structures and read succinct and understandable summaries about the brain.

So, grab your colouring pencils and get ready to colour, relax, and learn.

PS: If you are a complete beginner to learning brain anatomy, do not be put off by complex-looking terminology – you will become more familiar with these terms as you are guided through this book.

Chapter 1

How Our Brains Grow

Neurogenesis

So, let's start at the very beginning.

When you are conceived, you start off as a single fertilised egg. From then, the egg divides and produces a mass of identical stem cells (see key), which eventually leads to the formation of the foetus. Then, 9 months is up, and the baby is ready to be born into the world.

So, even before you are born, your cells have been hard at work creating the basic foundations of your brain. This process starts around 3 weeks after gestation and continues into early childhood. That being said, at almost any age, your brain is still subject to change, but we will get into that later.

For now, let's focus on this question: 'During pregnancy, what processes occur in order for a baby's brain to grow?'

- **Step One – Neurulation**
  At around 3 weeks after conception, the embryo has a spherical shape. The cells within this embryo (specifically in a region called the ectoderm) become thicker to form what is known as a 'neural plate'.

This plate then folds inwards on itself, as shown on page [xx]. This folding motion continues until it creates a neural groove. As this folding motion continues, the neural plate starts to form a tube, which is called the neural tube. The neural tube continues to grow and eventually closes at around week 6–7 of pregnancy.

- ***Step Two – Migration***
  This means exactly what it sounds like – the newly born neurons migrate to the different parts of the brain. Different neurons do different things in the brain, so they need to be in their respective destinations, ready for action when they are needed.

  So, the neurons have now arrived at their final destinations within the brain. From here, they have two options. They can either
  a. Become a mature neuron (i.e. go through changes that will make them effective brain cells) or
  b. Undergo programmed cell death (this is called apoptosis, whereby cells and neurons that are not needed are killed by other cells in the body).

  To become a mature neuron, they will grow spikey structures and a long tail, as shown in Chapter 3. We will get into the intricacies of neuronal communication later in the book, but, for now, we just need to understand that dendrites and axons grow on mature neurons to allow communication with other neurons. One other thing we need to know at this point is that neurons have a point of contact. This means that, when neurons want to talk to each other, they do so through a space between them called the synapse.

- ***Step Three – Differentiation***
  Once cells are in their correct place and begin to become mature neurons, there are a few more changes they need to go through before they are ready for action. Different neurons carry out different functions and so they need to have slightly different properties. For example, neurons that control our movement (motor neurons) need to have really long axons so they can relay their messages across the whole brain and body.

  So, in the differentiation stage, these minor changes within the neurons begin to form. The neurons are simply becoming specialised for the area they are going to be working in.

- ***Step Four – Synaptogenesis***
  At this point, specialised spaces are being formed ready for neuronal communication. Once one neuron talks to another neuron through the synapse, the synaptic space is 'activated'. For example, in the last trimester, a mother tends to feel the baby kick and move. The baby's neurons have been talking to each other to make the baby move, and so the synaptic space has been repeatedly activated.

- **Step Five – Synaptic Pruning**
  Lots of synapses are created in the brain and become activated through experiences such as hearing noises, feeding, and movement. However, while the baby is in the womb, not all of these synapses need to be there! After all, there is not much environmental stimulation in the womb. So, the synapses that the baby is repeatedly using, such as for feeding, movement, and hearing, will be allowed to stay. However, the synapses that go unused will be pruned via apoptosis.

- **Step Six – Myelination**
  As shown in Chapter 3, the long tail coming out of the neuron (axon) is coated in fat cells (myelin). The last stage of brain formation in the unborn baby's brain is myelination. The axons of the remaining neurons are wrapped in myelin to ensure they can communicate effectively.

We will get into exactly why dendrites, axons, and myelin aid communication on our neuron page. At this point, all we need to understand is that the neurons are getting ready for action.

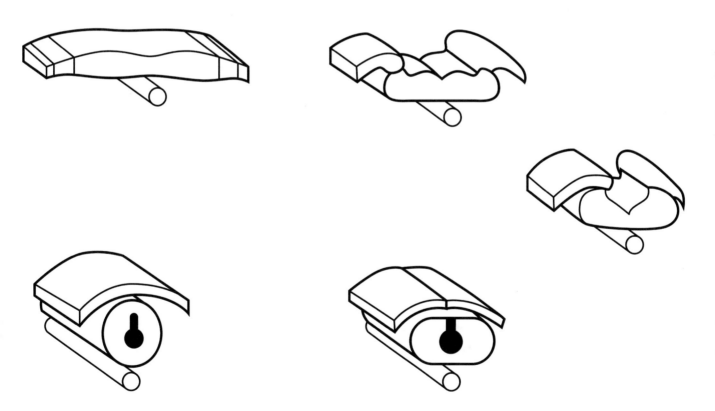

Chapter 2

Getting Started with Anatomy

Anatomical Position

Before we go into the intricacies of the human brain, it is important that you know some terminology that will help you navigate around the brain.

Like many parts of science, there are often a few words that mean the same thing. When you are reading textbooks and research papers, you will commonly hear the words

- Dorsal/superior
- Lateral
- Ventral/inferior

- Anterior/rostral
- Posterior/caudal.

Like any object, the brain can look different depending on which way you are looking at it. These words listed previously refer to the anatomical position from which you are viewing the brain.

Imagine you have put a brain on a table. The table is at your eye level, and you stand looking straight at the front of the brain. This is an **anterior view** of the brain.

You then walk around the table, so you are looking at the brain from the side. This is known as a **lateral view** of the brain.

You walk around the table once more and you are eye level with the back of the brain – this is a **posterior view**.

Now, imagine you climb on to a tall chair next to the table and look down at the brain. This is a **dorsal** or **superior view** of the brain.

Now just imagine that this table is made of glass. You crawl under the table and look up through the glass at the brain to get a **ventral view** of the brain.

Dorsal / superior

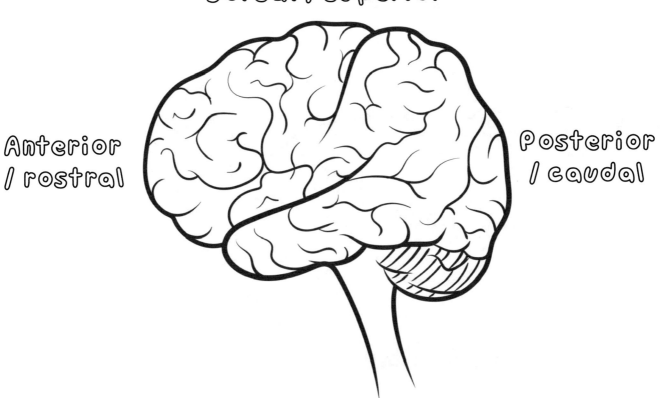

Anterior / rostral

Posterior / caudal

Ventral / inferior

Lobes of the Brain

Next, let's introduce the different lobes of the brain.

Just as your nose, stomach, and liver all carry out different functions, the same is true for different areas of the brain. There are four lobes in the brain that carry out a range of different functions which enable us to think, act, and behave in the way that we do.

These four lobes are:

- Frontal lobe
- Temporal lobe

- Parietal lobe
- Occipital lobe.

Neuroscience and psychological researchers have explored the roles of different brain areas, allowing us to come to a few general conclusions about the functions of each lobe.

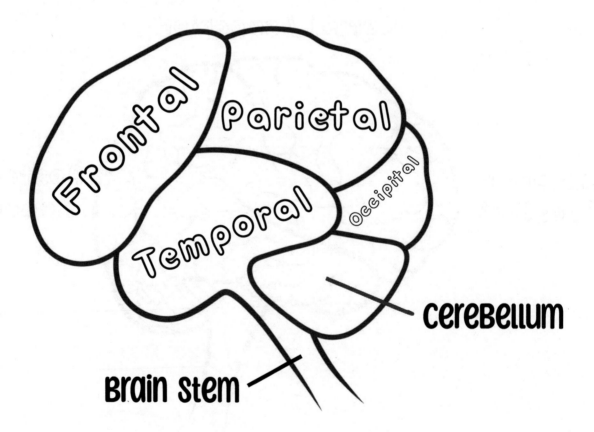

Functions of Each Lobe

Frontal

Voluntary movement
Planning
Attention
Working memory
Social behaviour
Reward
Impulsive control

Temporal

Memory
Understanding language
Recognition of auditory stimuli
Understanding verbal material
Face recognition

Parietal

Understanding spatial relationships
Touch perception

Occipital

Visual processing
Distance perception
Depth perception
Colour observation
Memory formation

Disclaimer! This is not to say that a single lobe carries out a single function. With the vast number of things our brains can do, a single lobe can be associated with many different functions. Also, a single function, such as memory, can be shared between different areas of the brain.

Brain Stem

The brain stem is one of the most important parts of our brains as it is responsible for the regulation of automatic functions that are essential to our survival. These include functions such as breathing, swallowing, and regulation of our heartbeat, blood pressure, and sleep cycle.

From the section on 'Lobes of the Brain', you can see that the brain stem is a small tube coming out of the bottom of the brain. This is because the brain stem connects the cortex to the spinal cord so that information can be relayed from the body to the brain.

It is therefore no surprise that the brain stem plays a vital role in consciousness, awareness, and movement.

As the brain stem is so vital to our survival, even minor damage to the brain stem can have drastic effects. This is because the brain and body cannot communicate as they should. Severe impairment of the brain stem can even lead to death, as it impairs our ability to carry out the important functions needed for survival.

The brain stem has three sections:

- Midbrain (mesencephalon): eye movement, visual and auditory processing, simple bodily movements;
- Medulla oblongata (myelencephalon): controls heartbeat, breathing, swallowing, sneezing; also plays a role in speech and memory;
- Pons (metencephalon): involved in sleeping, dreaming, and relaying information from the brain to the other parts of the brain stem.

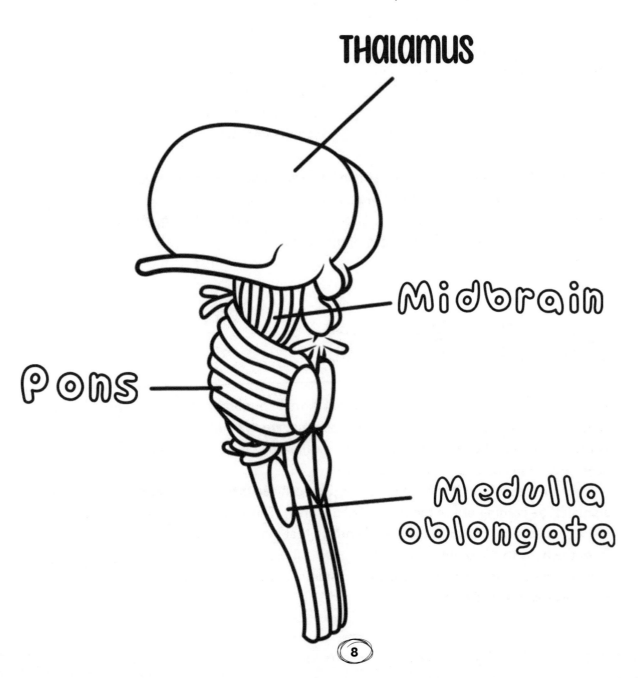

Limbic System

Researchers have known for decades that the structures deep within our brain play an important role in our behaviour. We call these deep structures the limbic system.

It is thought that the deeper structures in our brains are the parts that are most vital for our survival. The structures on the outside of our brain are still useful, but they are less important for the functions that keep us living and breathing.

Through years of research, we know a little more about exactly what each structure does. These conclusions are summarised below.

- **Thalamus**
  - Receiving sensory information from the nervous system and relaying it to the cortex
  - Interpretation of pain, temperature, and physical touch
  - Memory
  - Sleep–wake cycle
- **Corpus callosum**
  - Connecting the two hemispheres
  - Movement
  - Vision
  - Memory
- **Hypothalamus**
  - Releasing hormones for important physiological functions
  - Body temperature regulation
  - Regulation of mood
  - Regulation of sex drive
  - Sleep–wake cycle
  - Controls hunger
- **Pituitary gland**
  - Regulation of growth
  - Metabolism
  - Reproduction
  - Regulation of responses to stress
  - Lactation
- **Amygdala**
  - Interpretation of environmental threats
  - Regulation of fear response
  - Memory

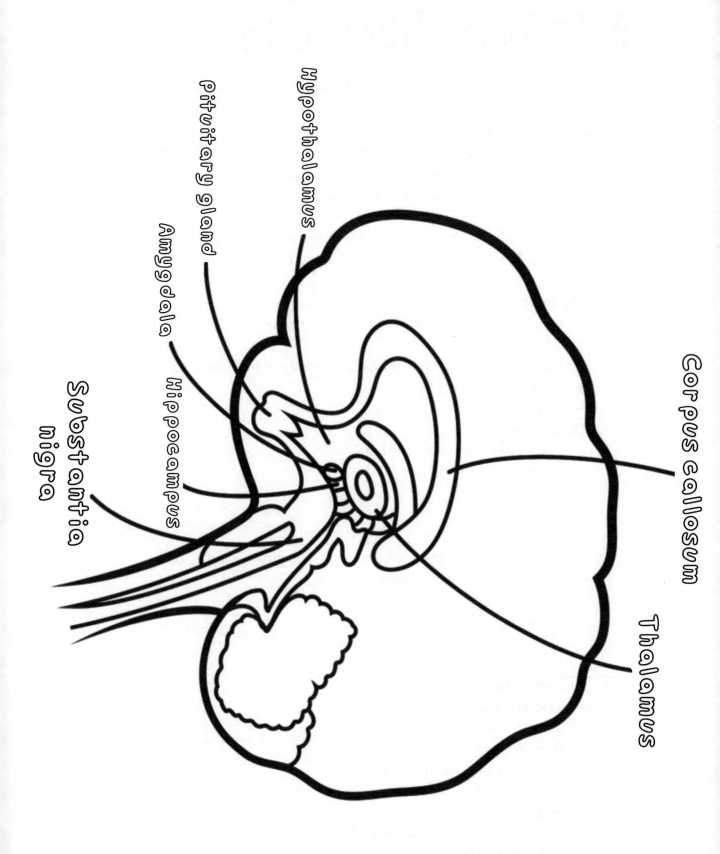

Hypothalamus

Pituitary gland

Amygdala

Hippocampus

Substantia nigra

Corpus callosum

Thalamus

- **Hippocampus**
  - Learning
  - Memory
  - Spatial navigation
- **Substantia nigra**
  - Production of neurotransmitter, dopamine
  - Control of movement
  - Learning
  - Regulation of mood
  - Judgement formation.

As you will be aware, the brain is a very complex organ – this means that there are many more structures in the brain that serve important functions!

However, the structures listed above include those that are most talked about in research and therefore will be most helpful to know for your studies.

Grooves, Gyri, Fissures, and Sulci

When you look at any picture of the brain, there are lots of little squiggles dotted around the whole cortex. These are not just pretty decorations for colouring books – they are very important!

They are called grooves, gyri, fissures, and sulci.

Whether they are called a groove, gyrus, fissure, or sulcus is dependent on how deeply they penetrate the cortex.

When learning brain anatomy, there are a couple of grooves, gyri, fissures, and sulci that you will need to know – mainly because we know about their functions and how important they are to our day-to-day living.

Some are particularly important because they separate different parts of the brain.

For example, the **central sulcus** separates the frontal and the parietal lobes, and the **lateral fissure** separates the temporal lobe from the frontal and parietal lobes (as seen in the first figure that follows).

The **interhemispheric fissure** separates the right hemisphere of the brain from the left hemisphere of the brain (as seen in the subsection on the 'Sagittal Plane').

The second figure shows a summary of some of the main grooves, gyri, fissures, and sulci that you will see in research articles and anatomy textbooks.

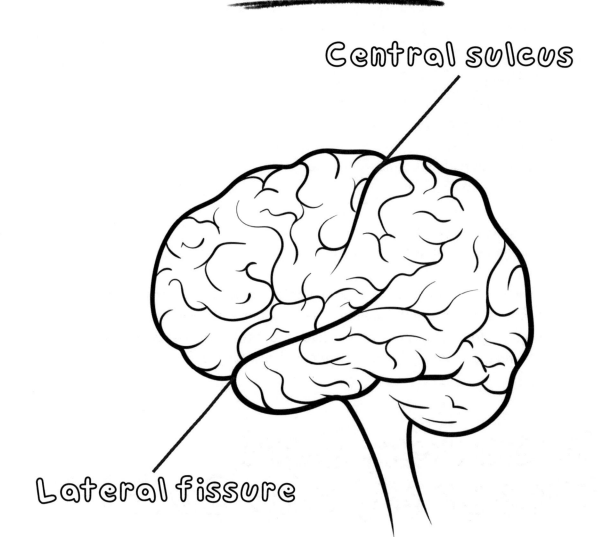

Central sulcus

Lateral fissure

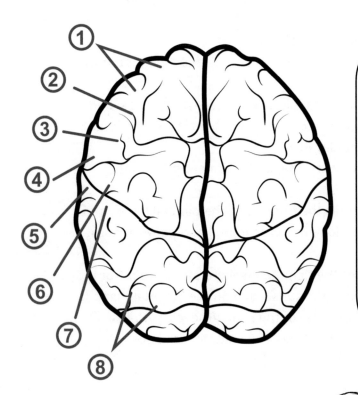

1) Superior frontal sulcus
2) Medial frontal gyrus
3) Precentral gyrus
4) Precentral sulcus
5) Central sulcus
6) Postcentral sulcus
7) Postcentral gyrus
8) Lunate gyrus

12

Coronal Cuts

Although scanning the brain can provide us with some information, some researchers cut the brain in various ways so they can look at the structures within the brain with their own eyes.

There are different ways in which the brain can be cut, known as sagittal plane, frontal plane, and lateral plane cuts. Each of these enables different parts of the brain to be seen.

Understanding the way in which the brain has been sliced is important to understand which brain structures the researchers will be looking at.

A sagittal plane cut cuts through the interhemispheric fissure, thereby dividing the right and left sides of the brain into separate parts.

Imagine you are looking at the brain from a lateral view. You find the central sulcus and cut straight downwards, dividing the brain into its anterior and posterior sections. This would be a **frontal plane cut**.

While still looking at the brain from a lateral view, cutting the brain left to right (or vice versa) is a **lateral plane cut**.

Of course, this is done on animal brains and post-mortem human brains for ethical reasons!

Sagittal Plane

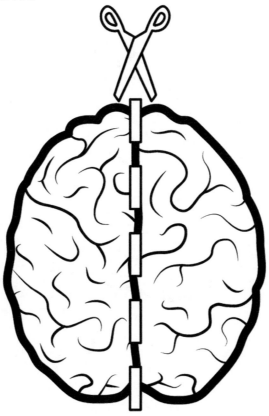

Lateral Plane

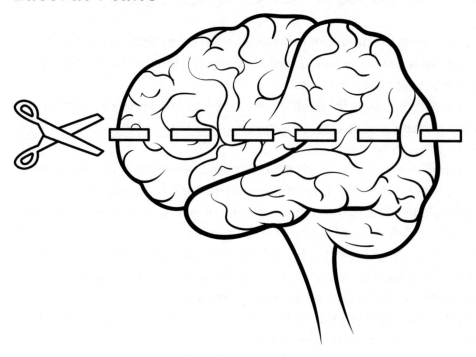

Frontal Plane

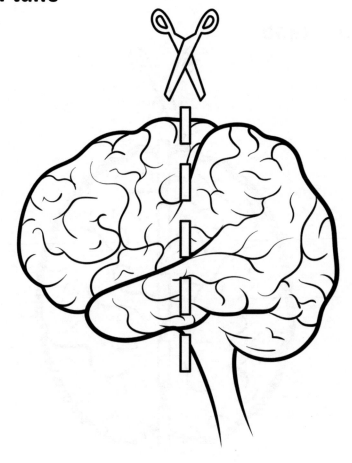

Chapter 3
Cells of the Brain

Neurons

Neurons are brain cells that send messages all over the body, including the brain, spinal cord, and the rest of the body. When neurons communicate with each other, they allow us to do near enough anything, such as walking, talking, and even breathing. They use electrical and chemical signals to communicate with each other. We have about 86 billion neurons, and they come in a variety of shapes and sizes.

As we mentioned in the neurogenesis chapter, there are different types of neurons in different areas of the brain. This is needed because the different neurons carry out different functions in their respective brain areas. But there are a few things that all neurons have in common.

They all have three main parts, as follows:

Cell Body/Soma

The main function of the cell body is to provide the neuron with a protective membrane, control cell activities, and provide energy for the neuron. The cell body contains a nucleus that houses the cell's genetic material. It also houses proteins that help the neuron survive. Inside the cell body, there are also specialised organelles that all work together to keep the cell healthy. These organelles are summarised below:

- Endoplasmic reticulum: this creates the proteins needed for neurotransmitter release (we will get into exactly what this is later);
- Ribosomes: these use genetic information to create proteins;
- Golgi body: this is known as the post office of the neuron. The proteins that are made by the endoplasmic reticulum are processed and sorted for transportation by the Golgi body. It also protects the neuron membrane by controlling which substances come in and out of the membrane.
- Mitochondria: these help the neuron have energy through metabolism.

Dendrites

The spikey structures coming out of the cell body are known as dendrites – dendrite literally means tree branch! The main role of dendrites is to receive information from other cells, ready to pass down the axon.

Just as the end of a tree branch has leaves, the ends of dendrites are covered in tiny spines that, in turn, are covered in synapses. This is so the dendrites can receive messages from other nearby neurons.

The number of dendrites on a neuron can vary depending on the type of neuron and its function in the brain.

Axon

The long tail coming from the cell body is called the axon and it is responsible for sending messages to other neurons. Neurons usually have one main axon. When a neuron decides it wants to send a message, an electrical signal is sent down the axon, ready to communicate with the dendrite of another nearby neuron.

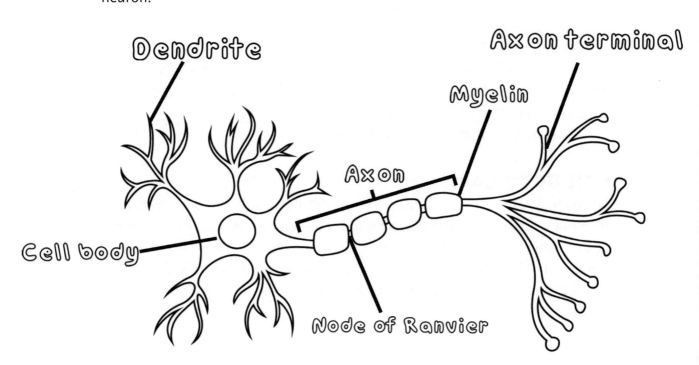

At the end of the axon, there is something called an **axon terminal**. It houses neurotransmitters, which are important communicators in the brain – we will get into this on the next page.

All we need to understand at this point is that the electrical signal that is needed for neuronal communication is sent down the axon. Because this electrical signal is so important, the axon has a few properties to help ensure that this signal can be sent effectively.

The axon is wrapped in a fatty substance called **myelin**. It protects electrical signals from being lost of interfered with. It's similar to the rubber wrapped around electrical wires to protect the wires and to keep them functioning properly.

Along the axon there are small gaps called the **nodes of Ranvier**. When an electrical signal is sent down the axon, the signal is able to jump over the nodes of Ranvier so it can get to the bottom of the axon as quickly as possible. This speeds up neuronal communication because the neuron can then pass the signal on to a nearby neuron in a timely fashion.

We've talked a lot about this 'electrical signal' that is sent from the neuron. Next, we need to understand how this electrical signal occurs, what it does to the neuron, and how this leads to neuronal communication.

Neurotransmission

So, at this point, we understand that neurons talk to each other in order for us to do things. They communicate via the synaptic gap between them. The neurons use electrical and chemical messengers to pass on messages to other surrounding neurons.

But how exactly does this happen?

When a neuron is resting (not being stimulated by other neurons), it is negatively charged. This electrical charge is known as the neuron's membrane potential.

But what happens when a nearby neuron wants to communicate with this resting neuron?

Remember, dendrites' main role is to detect communication from nearby neurons. So, when a nearby neuron wants to communicate with this resting neuron, the dendrites are the first to know about it.

As soon as the dendrites know that a nearby neuron wants to communicate, they tell the cell body. As we know, the cell body of the neuron has a membrane that allows particles to flow in and out. So, when the cell body knows that another neuron is talking to our resting neuron, it allows positively charged particles to flow into the neuron.

This causes the membrane potential to become more positive.

This positive electrical signal (action potential) is sent all the way down the axon. Remember, the main role of the axon is to transmit information to other neurons. You may also remember that, at the end of the axon, there are small sacks, called vesicles, that house neurotransmitters.

When the electrical signal reaches these vesicles, the neurotransmitters are released into the synaptic space.

It is at this point that neuronal communication changes from electrical signals to chemical signals.

Waiting on the other side of the synapse will be another neuron waiting to receive these neurotransmitters. So, the dendrites of another neuron will be there waiting to hear what this neuron wants to say.

In order to do this, they need to make contact with the neurotransmitters. So, on the dendrites of a neuron, there are specialised receptors ready to grab

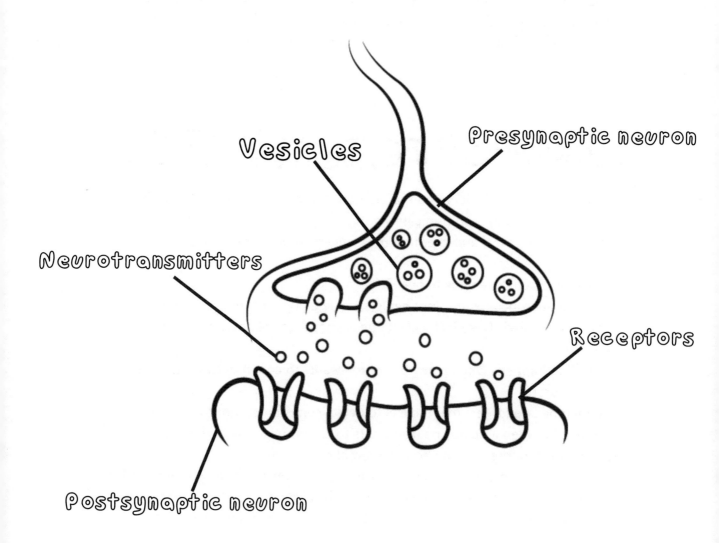

these neurotransmitters. When these neurotransmitters dock on to the receptors, the neuron receiving the information can decide how it wants to react.

Then, this process starts all over again in order for the next neuron to pass on more messages.

We call the neuron that releases the neurotransmitter the presynaptic neuron. The neuron that receives the neurotransmitter is called the postsynaptic neuron.

It is worth noting that not all of the neurotransmitters dock on to the receptors of the postsynaptic neuron. The presynaptic neuron sucks back all of the neurons that did not successfully dock on to a receptor on the postsynaptic neuron.

You may see the words 'depolarisation' and 'repolarisation' when reading about synaptic transmission.

The word depolarisation is just a fancy word to explain how, at the beginning of neuronal communication, the membrane potential becomes more positive than when in its resting state.

The word 'repolarisation' means that, after the neuron has let go of its neurotransmitters and successfully passed on the information, it eventually goes back to its resting state. This means that the membrane potential eventually goes back to normal, until another neuron is ready to communicate with it.

Blood-Brain Barrier

I hope you can see by now that the brain is an extremely precious organ. Just like anything precious, it should be protected!

Of course, our brain is protected in lots of ways. Our brains are encapsulated by our skull, which provides the brain with physical protection.

Our brain is also formed in three layers, called the meninges, which provide additional protection for the deeper structures of the brain and the brain stem. Remember, the brain stem is particularly vital for our survival and so it needs extra protection.

We also have something called cerebrospinal fluid that helps protect the brain. Our brain, brain stem, and spinal cord are coated in this clear, watery fluid that acts like a shock absorber in case of any trauma to the brain. It also helps get rid of any unwanted substances that could be damaging to our brain.

So, our brains appear to be well protected against physical trauma. But what about protecting the brain from toxins and pathogens that are already in our body?

This is the job of the blood–brain barrier! Its main role is to protect the brain from toxins, pathogens, inflammation, injury, and disease.

Blood pumps all around our body delivering the oxygen and nutrients needed for organ and tissue survival. But also circulating in the blood are toxins, pathogens, and inflammatory cells. If all these could just freely flow into the brain, the brain would be at risk of disease, injury, and inflammation, which could severely affect the functioning of the brain. The blood–brain barrier acts like a security guard for the brain. It stops certain molecules from entering, but allows in everything that is needed to help the brain survive.

We first found out about the blood–brain barrier in the 1960s. A researcher called Paul Elrich injected dye into the bloodstream of a mouse and found that this dye coloured all of the tissue in the mouse's body, apart from the brain.

Scientists later found that this is because of the blood–brain barrier – it did not let the dye into the brain. At that time, in the 1960s, microscopes weren't developed enough for scientists to actually see the blood–brain barrier. But, as science has developed, we are now able to see the blood–brain barrier, which can help us understand how it actually works.

When scientists were able to see the barrier, it was evident that there was a **physical barrier**.

Physical Barrier

Specialised cells that are usually found in blood vessels (endothelial cells) are so tightly packed together that they create 'tight junctions'. This makes it more difficult for molecules to be let in. These endothelial cells also have more mitochondria. This means that these cells are supplied with more energy to make sure they are always working as they should.

As scientists learned more about the blood–brain barrier, they learned that there are certain molecular properties that help it function.

For example, the endothelial cells that make up the physical barrier have more mitochondria, meaning a more efficient metabolism to ensure the cells always have energy to keep up their physical barrier.

The blood–brain barrier also consists of transporter proteins that act like security guards and only let certain molecules past once they know that they are safe. Cells within the blood–brain barrier, and the brain in general (we will cover these next), also communicate with other cells to ensure that the correct nutrients are being delivered to the barrier to keep it functioning.

So, as you can see, the blood–brain barrier is very selective in what it lets into the brain, using its physical barrier and its molecular properties. This usually works very well, but, in cases where the barrier becomes damaged, it can cause disease, stroke, multiple sclerosis, and brain trauma.

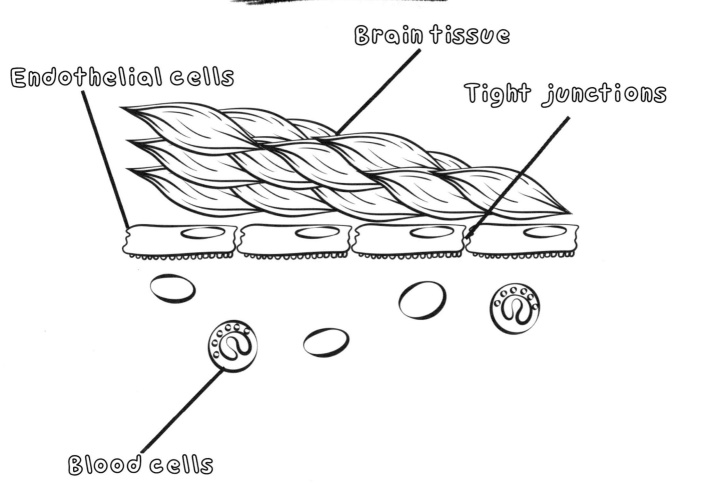

The fact that it is so hard for molecules to be allowed entry into the brain also poses an obstacle in drug design for the brain, as the blood–brain barrier prevents many molecules from being allowed into the brain.

Astrocytes

So, we have talked about how there are many functions in the brain that protect it from damage, such as the skull, meninges, cerebrospinal fluid, and the blood–brain barrier. But, as mentioned on the previous page, there are other cells that help our brain to keep functioning.

In the brain, we do not just have neurons. There are other cells in the brain that all work together to provide different functions.

One group of cells, called glial cells, are particularly important. We will cover three types of glial cells:

- Astrocytes
- Oligodendrocytes
- Microglial cells.

Let's look at astrocytes first. They get their name, 'astro', because they look a bit like stars. Unlike neurons, they do not use electrical signals to communicate with each other. They use complex molecular signals to interact and monitor the cellular environment in the brain.

We have covered synaptic transmission, and you may remember that, after the presynaptic neuron releases its neurotransmitters, not all are able to dock on to the receptors of the postsynaptic neuron. Some of these neurotransmitters are sucked back by the presynaptic neuron. However, sometimes there are still remaining neurotransmitters floating around in the synaptic space. Astrocytes play a role in helping the presynaptic neuron suck in the remaining neurotransmitters so that they can be recycled and stored back in their vesicles.

Astrocytes also help remove any damaging substances that are floating around in the cellular space.

We've also talked about the importance of the blood–brain barrier and its neuroprotective tasks. Astrocytes help regulate the blood–brain barrier. They do this by helping to co-ordinate blood flow in the brain, support immune functions, and help mitigate inflammation.

We now know the importance of axons and the role they play in neuronal communication. Astrocytes play a huge role in helping direct axons in the

right direction so they can communicate with the correct neurons effectively. Also, they are like first-aiders for axons whenever they become damaged. In the event of axon damage, astrocytes come along and help repair it as soon as possible so that the axon can get back to its job quickly.

They also help the brain maintain the correct pH – this helps to ensure that all the other cells in the brain have a perfect working environment so that they can all carry out their jobs.

Summary of Astrocyte Functions

- Help the reuptake and recycling of neurotransmitters;
- Remove anything that could potentially damage the brain (neuroimmune tasks);
- Help maintain the blood–brain barrier;
- Help axons by guiding them in the right direction;
- Act as first-aiders for axon repair;
- Maintain pH.

Oligodendrocytes

Another type of glial cell that is important in brain function is the oligodendrocyte.

Oligodendrocytes are specialised cells that generate and create myelin. Remember, myelin is the fatty substance that is wrapped around the axon of the neuron. Myelin helps speed up neuronal communication and helps signals to be sent to the correct neurons.

Oligodendrocytes are formed in the neural tube while the embryo is developing.

Research suggests that oligodendrocytes are activity-dependent. This means that the oligodendrocytes myelinate the axons that most need it – that is, the axons of neurons that are used the most.

For example, research suggests that oligodendrocytes are particularly active in myelination of the axons of neurons that are involved in movement (motor neurons). We move all the time, and so these neurons (and their axons) will be active all the time. Therefore, oligodendrocytes will gravitate more to these axons.

Being 'activity-dependent' also refers to how oligodendrocytes create myelin for neurons that need to be able to send responses quickly – for example, reflex responses such as flinching when a bug is flying towards you. In these situations, we need to be able to respond quickly, meaning the neurons need to communicate quickly. Therefore, oligodendrocytes will work hard to ensure these axons are myelinated.

One single oligodendrocyte can myelinate 50 axons – so they are very busy cells!

They also help the axon by providing metabolic support. After all, the axon is very long compared with the rest of the cell, so it may need an extra hand with maintaining its health. Research has found that oligodendrocytes tend to give the most metabolic support when an action potential is travelling down the axon. They look out for things called glutamatergic signals to see how well the axon is doing with its metabolism. If the axon needs a hand, oligodendrocytes are on standby waiting to help it out with its metabolism.

There is another specific type of oligodendrocyte called a satellite oligodendrocyte. Satellite oligodendrocytes are not thought to play a role in generating and creating myelin. They regulate fluid levels all over the brain, but they do step in when myelin becomes damaged. They help repair damaged myelin to ensure the neuron can work at its best.

Natural ageing of the brain shows a deterioration of myelin, but research is still investigating the lifespan of oligodendrocytes.

Research also suggests that oligodendrocytes can become damaged by excessive neurotransmitter release. This is why the role of astrocytes is so important – because they help get rid of the spare neurotransmitters that are floating around in the brain.

There are also some disorders that are linked to faulty or lack of oligodendrocytes, such as schizophrenia and bipolar disorder. It is thought that, when oligodendrocytes are not performing their myelination functions properly, it affects the way in which neurons communicate, resulting in psychiatric disorders.

Microglial Cells

Microglial cells also play a role in neuroprotection. They are created in the neural tube during development.

In the body, there is a certain group of cells called macrophages, which are a part of the body's immune system. When something damaging is floating around in the body – such as microbes, dead cells, or bacteria – the immune system becomes activated. The role of macrophages is to find whatever is causing this activation and then kill it.

Microglial cells are a type of macrophage. They are in the brain, waiting to strike when something damaging appears. This can be microbes, bacteria, or inflammatory cells that have sneaked through the blood–brain barrier. They also remove any dead cells that are no longer needed in the brain.

When microglial cells detect that there is something damaging in the brain, they can produce many cellular responses. This is so other cells can be recruited to help eliminate the damaging substance as quickly as possible.

Think of microglial cells as little vacuum cleaners that come around vacuuming up anything that could damage the central nervous system.

Remember we talked about how synapses that go unused are eliminated? This is thanks to microglial cells, as they eliminate these redundant synapses. For them to be able to do this, they need to monitor the synapses in the brain.

On the membranes of microglial cells, there are neurotransmitter receptors. This is so they can monitor the activity going on in the synapses to know which ones are functioning properly. If the microglial cells spot a synapse that is continually activated, they help strengthen it by talking to nearby neurons, astrocytes, and blood vessels to ensure that this synapse sticks around.

When they find a synapse that is redundant, they eliminate it. However, if they find a synapse that is used regularly, they help strengthen it. They particularly like to help strengthen synapses during development. They do this by talking to neurons, astrocytes, and blood vessels so they can all work together to keep the synapse functioning.

Remember, the dendrites are the part of the neuron that receives information from other neurons. If microglial cells see that the dendrites of a particular neuron are receiving lots of information, they help them out by increasing the dendrite density. This means that the microglial cells help the neuron to grow more dendrites to make sure they are taking in all the information from other cells.

You may be thinking, 'Wow, a microglial cell does so many things in the brain. How does it manage?'

Well, one thing about microglial cells is that they can change their shape depending on what function they are carrying out. This helps them to be able to complete their diverse range of tasks!

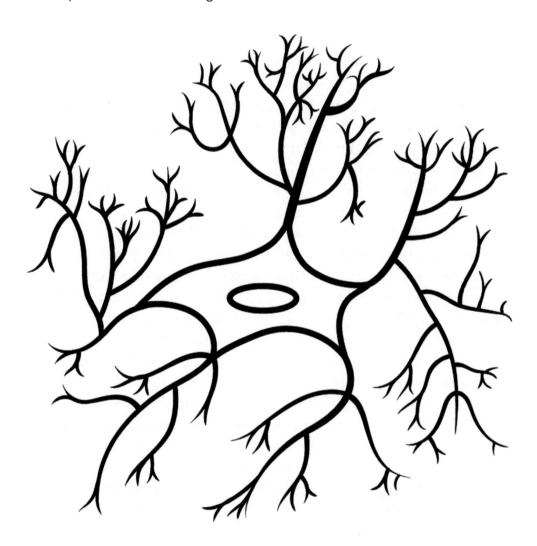

Chapter 4
Our Five Senses

Touch

Let's move on to how the brain processes the environment around us. We interact with the world through our five senses: touch, smell, sight, taste, and hearing.

Let's first look at how our brain processes the sensation of touch.

There are specialised receptors in the nerve endings that are skin and muscle. Once stimulated, they send an electrical signal to neurons around the spinal cord to let them know.

As you know, once a neuron becomes electrically stimulated, neurotransmitters are released from the presynaptic vesicle. The neurons we are talking about here are situated in the spinal cord.

Once the neurotransmitter has been released, the information is sent to the brain.

We have mentioned previously that there are different brain areas that are designed to process different things. This is the same for touch processing (somatosensory processing).

There is a specialised area of the brain called the somatosensory cortex that is dedicated to processing somatosensory information.

You will often see this brain area being described as a 'map'. This is because each body area has its own dedicated area on the somatosensory cortex. But

Somatosensory cortex

each body area does not have an equal dedicated space on the somatosensory cortex.

Parts of the body that are more sensitive will occupy a larger area, whereas the parts that are less sensitive will have a smaller dedicated area. This means that the somatosensory 'map' is based on sensitivity.

You can see that there is a funny-looking man in the illustration. This is known as a homunculus or 'little man'. This figure gives you a rough idea of which body parts occupy larger areas on the somatosensory cortex and which occupy smaller sections.

Some features of the homunculus, such as the lips and the hands, appear very large. This is because they occupy a larger section of the cortex. However, some features, such as the back, appear smaller – this is because they occupy a smaller section of the cortex.

You may be thinking, 'But the term "touch" is so broad. Surely it cannot be processed all in the same way?'

And you are correct.

We have many types of touch perception, such as temperature perception and pain sensation.

We said before that, when our body realises it has been touched, it is the neurons in the spinal cord that send the information up to the brain. Along this spinal cord, there are different routes that the messages can take. For example, if the nerve endings and neurons detect a painful stimulus, the message will take a different route up the spinal cord to relay this information.

Smell

There are all types of smells – good and bad. It is not just our nose that enables us to smell – we need our brains to process the odour.

An odour is made up of different molecules that make each smell different. When a smell is inhaled through our nose, sensory neurons are ready and waiting to take action.

On the membranes of these sensory neurons are receptors called odorant receptors. Each sensory neuron in the nasal cavity only has one type of odorant receptor. This means that only certain smells can activate certain sensory neurons.

So, we have different sensory neurons for different types of smells. We have around 4 million sensory neurons in the nasal cavity – all ready to detect specific scents from our environment.

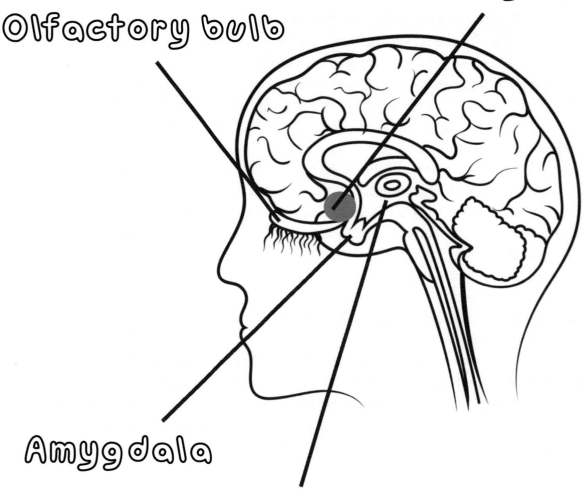

Olfactory cortex

Olfactory bulb

Amygdala

Hippocampus

When an odour is inhaled into the nose, the sensory neuron responsible for detecting this odour is activated. This happens once the molecules from the odour latch on to the sensory neuron's receptor.

Electrical signals are then relayed through the olfactory nerve to the brain to process the smell. Different electrical signals are sent to the brain depending on which sensory neurons have become activated.

Once the signals reach the brain, there is a mixture of instinctual and learned behaviour. For example, the brain will think 'is this smell a potential source of food?'. This is an instinctual behaviour.

The brain will also be processing 'Do I like this smell?' and 'Have I smelt it before?'. This is what we call learned behaviour.

The processing of the smell occurs in the olfactory cortex.

Have you ever noticed that your sense of taste and smell seem to be closely linked? For example, do you really love the smell of garlic cooking? Then, you may enjoy the taste of food dishes that contain garlic.

There is an explanation for this.

When you chew your food, molecules that help you smell are released and travel up your throat to your olfactory receptors at the back of your nose. So, the signals coming from your mouth meet with the signals from your nose in the olfactory bulb, ready to be sent up to your brain.

We all have our favourite smells. Some may love the smell of flowers, some may love the smell of a certain perfume, and some may love the smell of coffee being brewed in the morning. You can probably remember what your favourite smell smells like.

This is because your sense of smell and your memory are also closely linked. So, when signals from the olfactory bulb are being sent to the olfactory cortex, some of these odours are also sent to parts of the limbic system that govern memory, such as the amygdala and the hippocampus.

Our sense organs and the brain's structures are very good at working as a team to help us make sense of the world around us.

Taste

We bite, chew, and swallow lots of different types of food, and yet, somehow, they all manage to taste different.

So, how do we manage to perceive this sensation of taste?

It all starts with our tongue. If you stand in front of a mirror and stick your tongue out, you will be able to see tiny bumps on your tongue. Lots of people think these are your taste buds, which is partially correct.

The small bumps on your tongue are called papillae. Your taste buds actually lie underneath your papillae.

When you bite into food and begin to chew it, the food molecules mix with saliva and stimulate your papillae, which tell your taste buds to get ready to work.

There are five different primary types of taste: sweet, sour, salty, bitter, and savoury. Each little taste bud has its own receptors that can only detect one of these types of taste.

Let's say you bite into a lemon. The juice from the lemon mixes with your saliva and activates your taste buds. Only the taste buds that are designed to detect sour tastes will be activated. This means that your sour taste buds will have receptors on them to detect this sour lemon.

The taste buds then send messages to proteins that send electrically charged ions into the nerves to make sure that this message gets sent to the back of the mouth.

The message then gets sent up a tiny hole at the back of your mouth and travels to the gustatory cortex, where your brain will begin to process what it is tasting.

There are different parts of the gustatory cortex that will process different types of taste. In this case, the part of the gustatory cortex that processes sour tastes will become activated.

As was mentioned on the olfactory page, the senses of smell and taste give each other a hand to work out what we are both smelling and tasting.

Once our sour taste has reached the gustatory cortex and the taste has been processed, the gustatory cortex can send messages to other parts of the brain to react to the taste. For example, it may send a message to parts of the brain that deal with movement so that you can make a funny squinting face when you eat something sour.

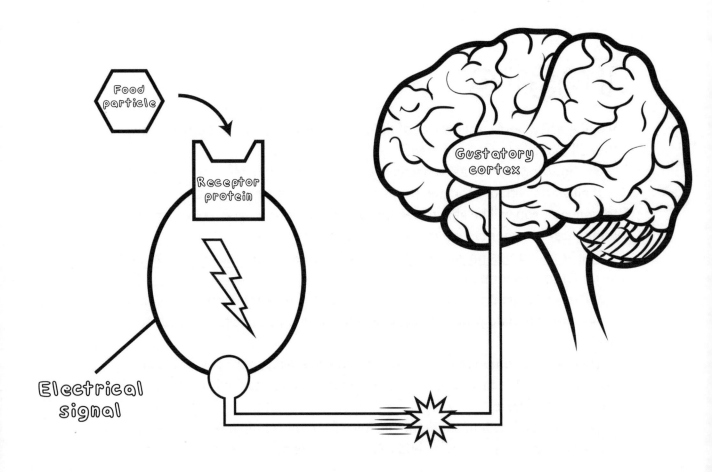

Now, if our brains are processing tastes of food in the same way, you may be wondering, how come you like the taste of salted crisps, but your sister hates the taste?

Well, researchers have found that this is actually to do with the sensitivity of your taste buds. Before your taste buds pass on their message, they add a little 'kick' to the taste. Some people have very sensitive taste buds, and so the taste may seem stronger to some than others. This explains why we have different likes and dislikes of food.

Sight

Our eyes are the window on to the world. They allow us to see the world around us, but it is our brains that really help us make sense of what we are looking at.

Our eyes are our sense organs for sight.

Specialised cells in the retina of the eye, called ganglion cells, send signals to the optic nerve. These signals then go to two separate parts of our limbic system, and, like most parts of the brain, these two areas serve two different functions.

- Signal 1 is sent to the thalamus (specifically in an area called the lateral geniculate nucleus). This is the main relay for visual processing. Here, the thalamus prepares the signals to be sent to the visual cortex for the visual stimuli to be fully processed. The thalamus is sensitive to basic visual stimuli, such as orientation of the object and whether it is dark or light.
- Signal 2 is sent to the superior colliculus. Here, visual stimuli are processed in order for us to control our bodily movements to react to the stimuli. For example, when you are reading this sentence, your eyes will be jumping to the next word. Your head orientation may also slightly change so that you can get the best possible view of the words. This is all thanks to the superior colliculus.

Signals from both the thalamus and the superior colliculus pass on their messages to the visual cortex. There are two different pathways along which these signals can be sent to the visual cortex – the 'what' pathway and the 'where' pathway.

The 'what' pathway contains signals that help us figure out what we are looking at.

The signals sent through the 'where' pathway help us figure out the movement and location of an object we are looking at.

These signals all reach the visual cortex where they will be further processed so we can really understand what we are looking at. The thalamus and the superior colliculus only process them in a very basic way; we need the visual cortex in order for us to fully understand the world around us.

The visual cortex is organised in a very specific way. Certain neurons are designed to process different properties of what we are looking at. For example, some neurons will be processing the colours of what we are looking at, some will be processing the texture, some will be processing the location, and so on. All these neurons will work together to form a comprehensive understanding of the visual world.

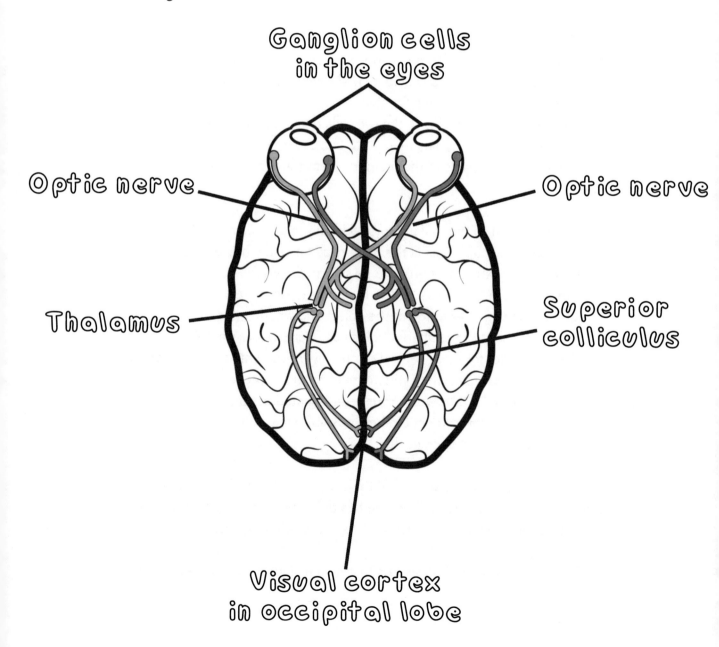

Ganglion cells
in the eyes

Optic nerve

Optic nerve

Thalamus

Superior
colliculus

Visual cortex
in occipital lobe

The neurons that are looking at the basic properties of the visual stimuli are situated closer to the bottom of the visual cortex, whereas the neurons that are processing the nitty-gritty, close-up details of the stimuli are closer to the top of the cortex. This is called a hierarchical arrangement.

It is worth noting here that there are lots of other cognitive processes needed for us to take in visual stimuli, such as attention. So, the visual cortex does not work alone!

Hearing

Our response to the sounds around us plays a huge role in our behaviour. Sounds can warn us of danger, such as a car coming when we are crossing the road. But sound also helps us interact with our environment, such as when we listen to others in conversation.

When we hear a noise, the hair fibres in our cochleae become activated. The cochlea is a small structure inside our ear.

When a noise has been detected, electrical signals are sent to the auditory nerve, which sends this information to a part of the brain called the auditory cortex. This is where the sound will be processed. We can then decide how we want to react to the noise around us.

On the way to the auditory cortex, the signal stops off at the brain stem. The brain stem will process the basic properties of the sound such as its duration, intensity, and frequency. Researchers seem to think that this process acts as a survival instinct. The message is being 'checked' by the brain stem to see if we need to produce a reflex such as turning our head away from the noise.

On the way to the auditory cortex, the signal also stops at the thalamus. Here, the brain processes the sound to see if we need to produce a motor response, such as covering our ears, moving away from the noise, or producing a social response. For example, if you hear your friend call your name from behind you, the thalamus is there to prepare you to turn around so that you can greet your friend.

The auditory cortex is responsible for further processing of the sounds that we hear. You may see the auditory cortex being described as a 'frequency map'.

This is because different sound frequencies are processed in different parts of the auditory cortex. So, specific neurons in the auditory cortex are designed to become activated for different ranges of frequency.

The cochlea is also designed as a frequency map, and so audio messages will come from specific parts of the cochlea to specific parts of the auditory cortex.

The auditory cortex will also process where the sound is coming from. It will send messages to the frontal lobe and other structures of the brain so that we can think about things like:

- Have we heard this sound before?
- What does it mean?
- Do we like this sound?

As we can see again, brain areas are all working together to make sense of the world around us.

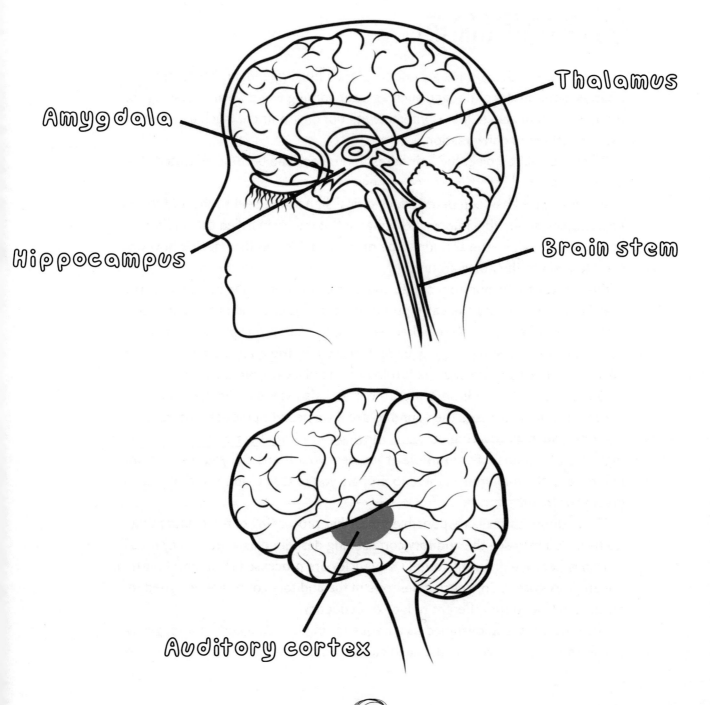

Chapter 5
Important Functions

Memory

We rely on our memory so much. It gives us context for the world around us and helps us learn based on previous experiences.

We have different stages of memory, such as interpreting and 'taking in' information, storing it, and then retrieving it when we need it.

We create a mental image of certain events so that we can access them when we need them.

Research suggests that we have different types of memory. These include:

- Sensory memory: that is, things we have just taken a quick glance at but have not really 'remembered';
- Short-term memory: remembering things we may need for that specific moment – for example, remembering which junction we need to take off the motorway;
- Long-term memory: things that we can remember from the past and can retrieve at any moment – for example, your mum's maiden name, the name of your first pet, and the name of the school you went to.

It is thought that information goes through your short-term memory and then into your long-term memory.

You may have a favourite childhood memory stored in your long-term memory and you may think about this often. Each time you think about it, you are strengthening the neural networks that allow you to remember the information from the event.

This is also how you form habitual behaviour. For example, many people who drive can do so without really having to 'think' about it. They can change gear with ease and can operate the pedals without intense concentration. This is because this neural network has been activated so often that the memory of how to drive a car comes to them with ease.

We have 'knowing what' memories (declarative memories), such as remembering that Rome is the capital of Italy. We also have 'knowing how' memories, such as knowing how to swim and drive.

Memories can also be affected by our emotions. For example, some memories may be 'happy memories', and so we will think about them more, strengthening the neuronal connections. However, we may have some negative memories that we try not to think about; because they are not thought about,

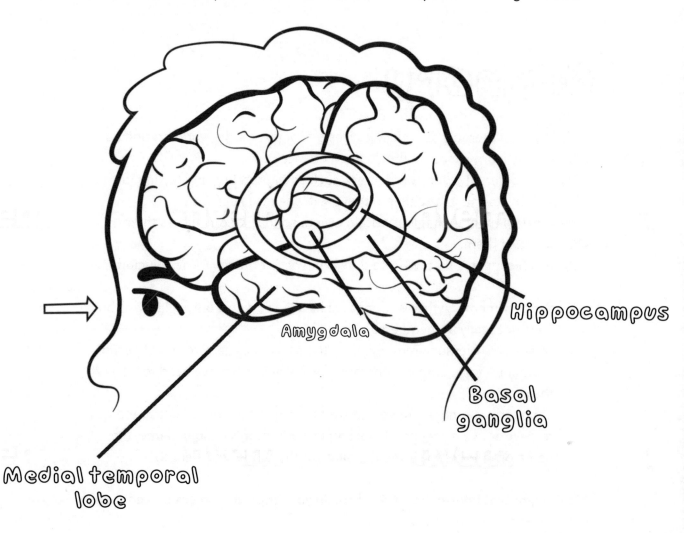

Hippocampus

Amygdala

Basal ganglia

Medial temporal lobe

they become activated less often, and so the memories of the events become less clear.

Because there are lots of different stages to memory and also lots of different types, there are lots of brain areas involved. The most important ones are summarised below.

- Hippocampus: helps our memories go from short-term memory to long-term memory by additional processing; it is especially involved in remembering events that have happened to you and semantic memories such as recalling words and facts;
- Frontal cortex: helps us think about and consolidate our memories;
- Medial temporal lobe: storage of declarative memories;
- Amygdala: helps with the emotional processing and consolidation of memories;
- Basal ganglia: helps consolidate implicit/motor memories.

Stress

The feeling of stress is caused by a cascade of hormones that produce physiological changes in our body.

For example, when you are stressed, you may feel like your heart is pounding out of your chest, your muscles may feel tense, and you may begin to sweat.

When we are experiencing stress, we are in 'fight/flight' mode. This means that our body is getting ready to either 'fight' the stress or run away from it. Scientists seem to think that this is a survival mechanism that is built into our brains.

But, in the modern day, we may 'overreact' to stimuli that pose no real physical threat. For example, we may feel stressed when we are about to give a public speech. There is usually no physical danger, but our bodies are still going into the 'fight/flight' mode, as it is our instinctual reaction to stress.

When we encounter stress, the amygdala is the first to know about it. If the amygdala thinks that there is a reason for us to be stressed, it tells the hypothalamus to take action.

The hypothalamus is the command centre as it can send messages all over the body to order the release of specific hormones.

When the hypothalamus becomes active, this activates our autonomic nervous system (specifically the sympathetic nervous system), which causes activation of the pituitary gland and our adrenal glands.

This causes a release of adrenaline in the body that is pumped through the blood to produce the physiological changes that we see when we are under stress.

Adrenaline then causes the release of glucose and fats from temporary storage sites in our body, so that we have enough energy to fight the stress.

If our brain thinks we are in danger, the activation of the hypothalamus will also cause the release of corticotrophin hormone. This then travels to the pituitary gland as an additional warning sign. Once this warning sign has reached the pituitary gland, adrenocorticotrophin hormones are released, which then tell the adrenal glands to produce the hormone cortisol. This gives us additional energy to fight the stress.

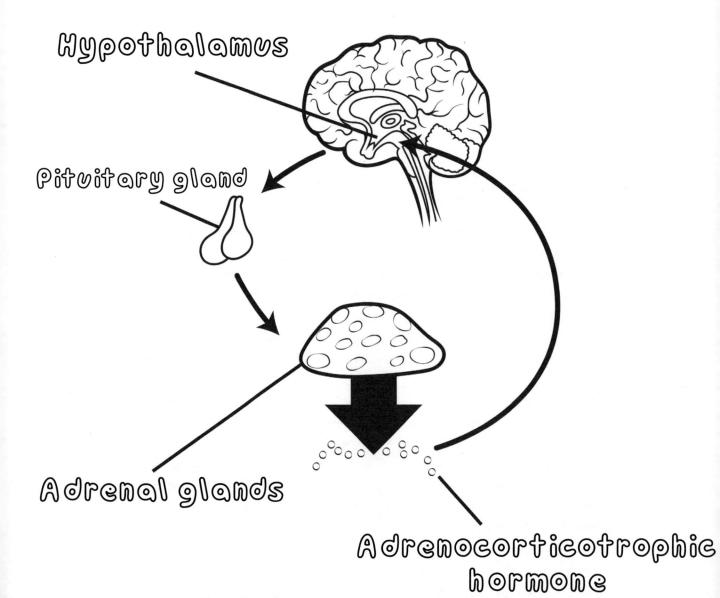

Hypothalamus

Pituitary gland

Adrenal glands

Adrenocorticotrophic hormone

Our autonomic nervous system is split into two separate systems:

1. The sympathetic nervous system: this acts like an accelerator pedal in a car. It activates our body and gives us a burst of energy so that we can combat the stress described above.
2. The parasympathetic nervous system: this is known as the 'rest and digest' system. It helps the body calm down after periods of stress and acts like a brake for the sympathetic nervous system by slowing down the release of hormones.

Sleep

Our sleep is so important – we spend one-third of our time on Earth asleep.

The amount of sleep we have is not the only important factor. We need good-quality sleep at the right times of the day for us to function at our best.

Without sleep, we cannot form or maintain important pathways in the brain.

I'm sure you can think about a time that you have felt very sleep-deprived. You may have found it difficult to concentrate and to respond quickly to situations. This is because sleep is vital for neuronal communication in the brain.

While you are fast asleep, your brain is working hard to remove toxins from your brain, which helps it function properly when you wake up from your sleep.

We have different stages of sleep, meaning our brain's activity varies throughout the night. We move through these different stages multiple times in the night. See below for a summary of these stages!

But, how does your body know when it needs to sleep and when it should be awake?

It is all down to something called your circadian rhythm. It's your body's way of regulating when you need to sleep and when you should be awake. This is usually based around a 24-hour time frame.

Your circadian rhythm is responsible for controlling your body temperature, metabolism throughout the day, and release of different hormones. This helps your body control its timing of when you need to sleep.

Your circadian rhythm also links to the environment by measuring light and temperature.

Specialised cells within the eyes process the amount of light; this then tells the brain whether you should be feeling sleepy or not. Throughout the day, your brain releases a certain neurotransmitter called adenosine. As more adenosine builds up in the brain throughout the day, you begin to feel sleepier.

I'm sure most of you have had a cup of coffee, particularly when you are feeling tired, and it has seemed to make you feel more awake. This is because caffeine counteracts the function of adenosine.

While there are lots of brain areas that play a role in our sleep cycle, the important ones are summarised below:

- The thalamus: this also 'goes to sleep' – that is, it is not active – when we are in non-REM sleep; in REM sleep, it relays information about colour, sounds, and sensations that help us fill our dreams;
- The pineal gland: this increases production of the neurotransmitter melatonin when it is dark (this helps us sleep);
- The amygdala: this processes our emotions during REM sleep.

So, as you can see, while you are sound asleep, your brain is still very active!

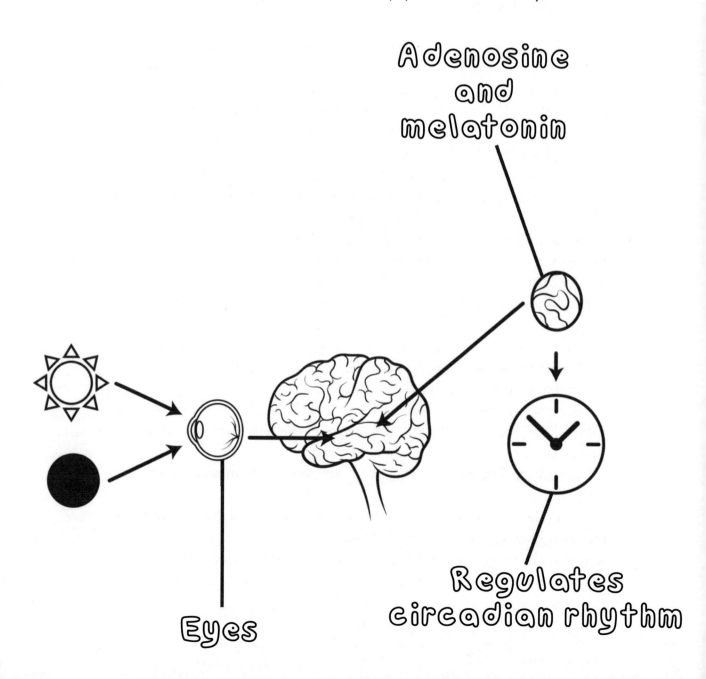

Language

Research has looked into language in the brain for a long time. We are social beings – we like to communicate! Therefore, language is a vital function of the brain.

The term 'language' has many different subgroups. For example, for us to fully utilise our language, our brain must be able to:

- Learn new words;
- Understand the words of others;
- Articulate our words (speech production);
- Use phonetics to spell out words.

All of this is closely linked to our long-term memory (see our memory page!)

When we are born, we do not have the ability to speak. But, in fact, babies are born with preconditions for learning language. They are able to hear noises from outside the womb and have their own methods of communicating that they want something, such as crying.

The brain areas that we know are involved in language are already formed in the brain when a child is born, but it is through interaction with the environment that these neural structures really become active.

Lots of brain areas are involved with language production. For example, you must be able to think about what you are going to say and must be able to move your tongue and mouth to speak.

There are two important areas when it comes to speech production and language processing. These are

1. Broca's area: this is situated in the frontal lobe and is important in speech production and articulation of words;
2. Wernicke's area: this is located in the left temporal lobe and is involved in language processing.

Both of these areas are linked together by a bundle of nerve fibres called the arcuate fasciculus.

Research has shown that damage to either of these areas can severely affect language function. For example, if you have damage to Wernicke's area, you may have difficulty comprehending language but have no issues with the production and articulation of speech.

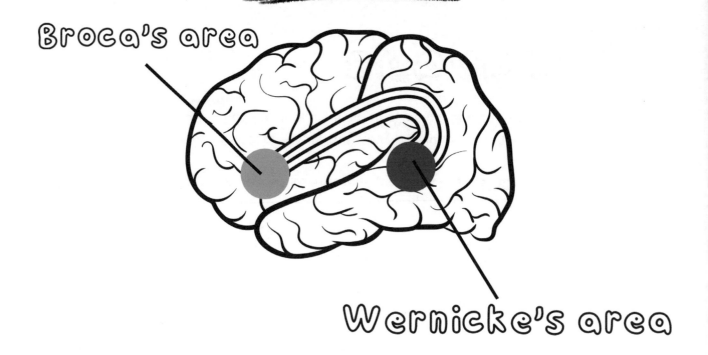

Broca's area

Wernicke's area

However, if you have damage to Broca's area, you may not be able to articulate properly but will still be able to understand other people.

So, although these two areas are linked by nerve fibres, they do seem to work independently.

Movement

We move our bodies all the time – whether voluntarily or involuntarily. These movements allow us to carry out our day-to-day activities and help us survive.

For example, you can voluntarily pick up a mug when you want a sip of your drink. Your motor cortex sends messages to your brain stem, along the spinal cord, and this results in muscle command. Your brain tells your muscles to move once you have decided to complete an action.

We also have involuntary movements, such as your stomach moving to help digest food. These movements that help us survive are usually controlled by the hypothalamus (see our endocrine system page).

It's not all about moving our limbs to complete actions. We are constantly moving, whether we notice it or not, such as moving our head and eyes to explore the world around us or moving our face to form different facial expressions.

As we move in so many ways, lots of different brain areas are involved. For example, if we want to pick up a mug, we have the goal of picking up the mug by the handle and bringing the mug towards our mouth. For this goal-directed behaviour, the parietal lobe will be activated.

We may also use our memory when carrying out motor movements. For example, if you go to kick a football, you may think about the times you have kicked a ball in the past. You may kick a ball with your right foot, using the side of your shoe and with a certain amount of force based on your previous experience of kicking a ball. Therefore, your 'memory' parts of the brain may be involved in your movement.

However, there are a few brain areas that are vital to our motor movements. These include:

- The motor cortex: this kickstarts the signal sending process;
- The premotor cortex: this plans and co-ordinates our movements;
- The primary motor cortex: this sends a message from the brain to the brain stem and spinal cord; this message is then sent to the muscles that enable us to move.

Information is not just sent from the brain to the body. There is a feedback loop – the body is able to send information about movement from the muscles back to the brain.

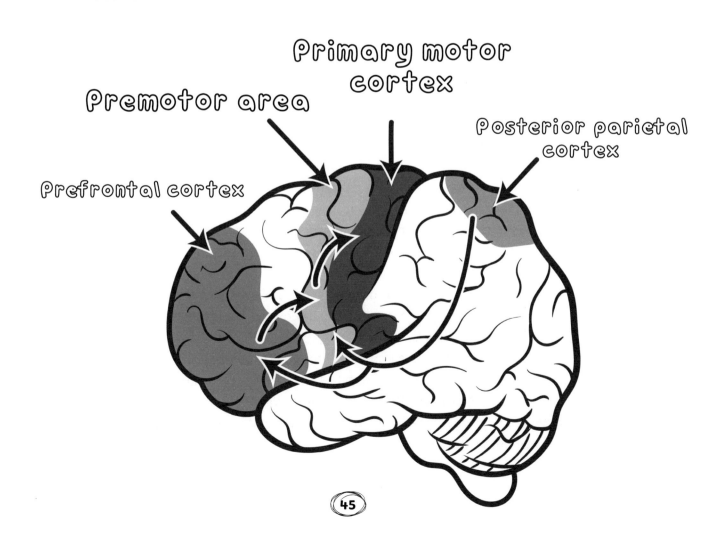

Consciousness

I'm sure you have heard of the terms 'consciousness' and 'unconscious' before.

For example, a person in a coma after a traumatic injury to the head may be 'unconscious', yet their bodily functions such as breathing are still working. The person may be completely unaware of their surroundings, as if they are in a really deep sleep, but they are still alive.

What structures in the brain govern this state of 'consciousness'?

This has been researched for a very long time, and there is a lot of controversy about exactly which areas govern your conscious state.

Scientists tend to categorise consciousness in two broad categories:

1. The state of consciousness wakefulness: this would include things like having basic reflexes such as sucking, swallowing, and the ability to open your eyes;
2. The content of conscious awareness: this refers to complex thought processes, being able to 'take in' your environment and really understand what is going on around you.

The fact that the definition of consciousness is segregated in such ways makes it a difficult phenomenon to study.

For example, a person may open their eyes, be able to breath and swallow. However, they may not have substantial content of awareness. This means that they may not do things such as taste their food or feel pain.

So, are they conscious or not? They have a state of wakefulness, but little content of conscious awareness.

If a person has reduced content of awareness, you might describe them as being in a vegetative state. They are not 'taking in' the environment, such as experiencing taste or having complex thought processes.

There are a few areas of the brain that have been linked to consciousness. There appears to be no 'seat' of consciousness, but rather lots of brain areas working together to keep you in a conscious state. These include:

- The brain stem: basic functions such as breathing, sucking, and swallowing are all needed to keep us alive and, therefore, are important for our state of consciousness.
- The claustrum: some researchers (although it is controversial) describe the claustrum as the seat of consciousness. It receives messages from all over the brain and helps synchronise them; it is suggested that the claustrum is how we piece together all the information around us to enable a substantial content of awareness.

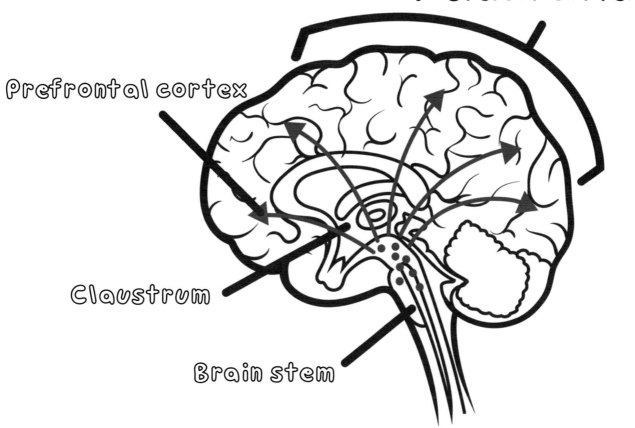

Posterior cortex

Prefrontal cortex

Claustrum

Brain stem

- The posterior cortex, including the temporal and occipital lobes: these are the main parts of the brain that process sensory information such as noise and sight. Since consciousness is described as being aware of our surroundings, it makes sense that the posterior cortex is heavily involved in our consciousness.

But, in reality, there are many other brain areas that are involved in our consciousness. For example, our prefrontal cortex allows us to have complex thought processes, such as thinking about the information we are taking in.

It may be that we cannot pinpoint specific areas that govern consciousness, as brain areas work together as a whole to enable our consciousness.

Endocrine System

We have hormones that float around our whole body. They are chemical signals that help our body function. For example, they help with growth, metabolism, sexual function, menstrual cycle, fertility, and mood.

But these hormones don't just act on their own – they need to be told! And this is the job of the brain. Our brain tells various glands in the body to start producing hormones when they are needed.

Two areas of the brain are particularly important in telling these glands to work:

1. The pituitary gland: this acts as a hormone level detector. This means it receives messages from all over the body regarding hormone levels. When it receives a message that a hormone level is too low or too high, it tells the hypothalamus.
2. The hypothalamus: this is able to excite or inhibit the production of hormones in different glands in the body. So, once the pituitary gland tells the hypothalamus that we need more or less of a certain hormone, the hypothalamus will send messages to the glands to ensure that these levels return to normal.

Hormone levels can change depending on the food we eat, the time of day, or the menstrual cycle, among many other factors. The pituitary gland is always active to keep an eye on these ever-changing levels.

The job of the hypothalamus is to maintain the perfect number of hormones so that all of our other organs can function properly. We call this 'homeostasis' – the tendency to always keep a 'perfect' environment in the body – that is, keeping the hormone levels just right!

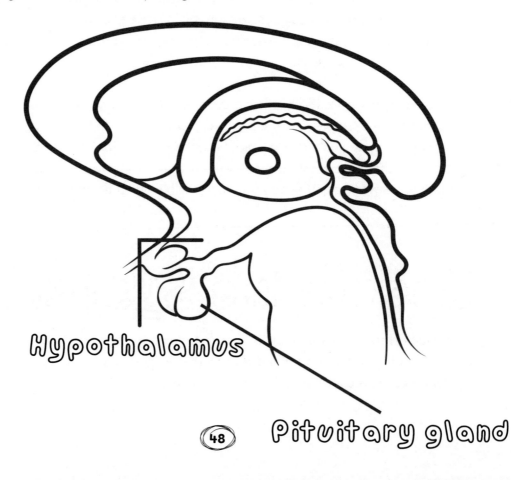

Hypothalamus

Pituitary gland

48

Chapter 6
Disorders

Stroke

A stroke is defined as when something blocks the blood supply in the brain. It can cause damaging effects to the brain because the oxygen supply is impeded, which causes the death of neurons and damage to brain areas. It can cause long-lasting brain damage, long-term disability, or death.

Symptoms

The onset of a stoke can have very specific symptoms, such as weakness in the face, difficulty moving limbs, slurred speech, and vision problems. You can memorise these using the acronym F.A.S.T (facial drooping, arm weakness, speech difficult – time to call for help).

After a stroke has occurred, there can be long-lasting effects that depend on which brain area has had depleted levels of oxygen. These can include paralysis/loss of movement, speech problems, issues swallowing and chewing food, memory loss, mood swings, and changes in behaviour.

Causes

A stroke can happen for two reasons:

1. An artery in the brain becomes blocked (ischaemic stroke): this stops blood being pumped through the brain. Blood carries oxygen and nutrients that are needed for the neurons to survive. Without this oxygen, even for a short period of time, neurons begin to die.
2. An artery bursts (haemorrhagic stroke): when the artery bursts, the blood cannot travel through its usual pathway to reach areas of the brain, resulting in the brain areas being deprived of oxygen. It also means that

blood leaks out of the arteries, which puts pressure on the brain and can further damage it.

Ischaemic strokes are the most common and can be caused by narrowed blood vessels. This can happen when fatty deposits build up in the artery over time. They can also be caused by clots or other debris in the blood.

Sometimes, an ischaemic stroke can lead to a haemorrhagic stroke. This is when the artery becomes blocked, and pressure builds up inside the artery to the point where the artery ruptures.

A haemorrhagic stroke is linked to uncontrolled blood pressure, overuse of blood thinning medication, trauma, or unnatural bulges in the arteries.

As we know, blood pumps all around the brain, and so strokes can occur anywhere in the brain. Where the stroke occurs has a direct impact on the symptoms, as different brain areas will be affected depending on which brain area the stroke occurred in.

There is also another type of stroke called a transient ischaemic attack (TIA), which is also known as a 'mini-stroke'. This is when the oxygen supply to an area of the brain is depleted for a short period of time but is then restored in less than 5 minutes. TIAs do not cause permanent damage to the brain but do serve as a 'warning sign' that there could be future risk of stroke. Therefore, following a TIA, a patient will usually be put on medication to minimise the risk of another TIA or future stroke.

Treatment

It is important that you act fast when you suspect that someone is having a stroke. Once the brain area has become damaged, there is not much that can be done if the neurons have already died.

The first thing a clinician will do if they suspect that someone is having an ischaemic stroke is administer something called a plasminogen activator. This is a type of medication that will break down clots, which will help clear the artery that is blocked. Blood can then flood back into the brain area and deliver oxygen as quickly as possible. Research has shown that this is only effective up to 3 hours after the first symptoms appear. This is why it is important to act fast.

After a person has had a stroke, there are a number of preventative measures that will be put in place to ensure they do not have another. These include medication to prevent and dissolve blood clots, blood pressure medication, and medication to reduce cholesterol (to minimise the fatty deposits in the arteries).

Ischaemic

Plaque / debris

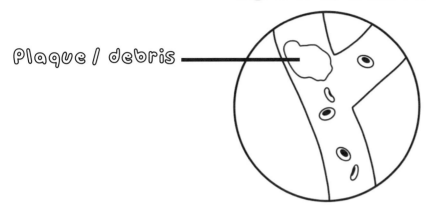

Haemorrhagic

Burst artery

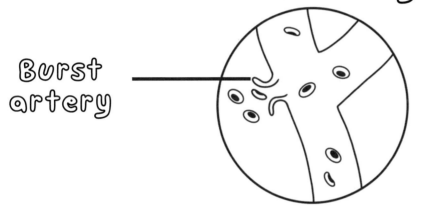

Transient ischaemic attack

Plaque / debris

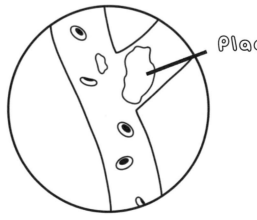

Parkinson's Disease

Parkinson's is a neurodegenerative disease that is characterised by the progressive loss of dopamine-producing neurons. As we know, dopamine is involved in controlling our movement. So, damage to dopamine neurons can cause issues with movement.

The symptoms get worse over time because, as more neurons die, it is more difficult for new dopamine to be produced. This means that, over time, there will be less and less dopamine in the brain, which is why symptoms get worse.

Symptoms

Symptoms tend to be mild at the beginning of the disease. Patients may notice small tremors in their hands, even when they are relaxing. They cannot control or stop these tremors. Slowness of movement is another main symptom, which is referred to as bradykinesia.

Patients may feel that their muscles are stiff, which can be painful for them – we call this pain dystonia.

Because dopamine carries out so many different functions in the brain, the loss of dopamine can cause a wide range of other symptoms. These can include:

- Poorer sense of smell
- Bladder and bowel problems
- Dizziness
- Swallowing difficulties
- Problems with sleeping
- Depression and anxiety
- Cognitive impairment.

Causes

We know that the onset of Parkinson's is due to progressive loss of dopamine in the brain, but we don't actually know why these neurons begin to die.

Dopamine loss tends to start in a part of the brain called the basal ganglia – specifically in a region called the substantia nigra.

The decrease in dopaminergic neurons causes a cascade of effects where dopamine production and release are hindered.

Treatment

As we don't know why the dopamine neurons are dying, a treatment has not been found to stop this death from occurring.

However, some treatments are available to increase the levels of dopamine in the brain in order to relieve the symptoms of Parkinson's and slow down the progression of the disease.

The most common treatment is a medication called levodopa.

Remember how we talked about the blood–brain barrier and how it offers molecules selective access into the brain? Well, this actually poses a problem for treating Parkinson's. We cannot give patients 'pure' dopamine because the blood–brain barrier will not allow it to enter the brain.

So, levodopa is what we call a 'precursor' of dopamine. The blood–brain barrier lets this precursor into the brain. Once in the brain, levodopa helps the brain produce more dopamine.

Levodopa is usually taken with another medication called carbidopa. This helps ensure that the body does not breakdown the levodopa molecules before they have a chance to reach the brain.

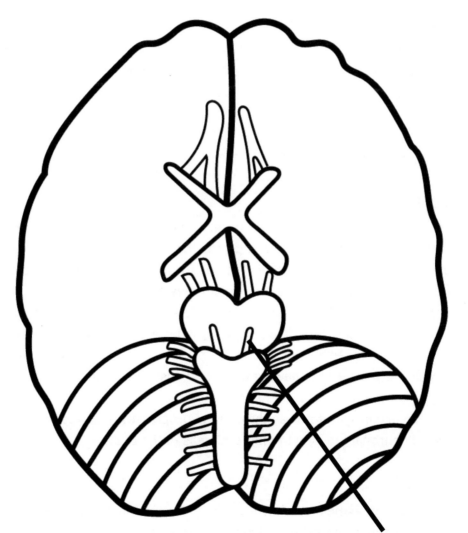

Substantia nigra

Alzheimer's Disease

Alzheimer's is a neurodegenerative disease that results in the progressive loss of neuronal function. Neurons either become damaged or they die, causing neuronal networks to fail and resulting in progressive brain shrinkage (brain atrophy).

The survival of neurons is based on three important factors:

- The neuron's ability to communicate (if you don't use it, you lose it!);
- The metabolism of the neuron (it needs energy to be able to pass on information);
- Repair (if the neuron becomes damaged, it needs to be repaired or it will not be able to communicate or metabolise properly).

Alzheimer's appears to impact all three of these factors, which explains the progressive injury to and death of neurons.

When we think of Alzheimer's, most people associate it with memory loss. This is because neuronal death appears to begin in parts of the brain associated with memory, such as the hippocampus. In the later stages of the disease, this neuronal death starts to happen in other parts of the brain. There appears to be no pattern in which Alzheimer's spreads. This means that each individual will have a different pattern of neuronal death.

Symptoms

As neuronal death occurs in different parts of the brain for different people, this means there is a diverse range of symptoms that can be observed in Alzheimer's.

The first symptoms of Alzheimer's include forgetfulness, having trouble thinking of the right word, and asking questions repeatedly.

As the disease progresses, you can expect to see increased confusion, delusions, issues with sleep, mood swings, and issues with spatial awareness.

In the later stages, Alzheimer's patients may experience difficulty moving, issues with swallowing and chewing their food, loss of speech, and worsening of memory.

The difference in symptoms as the disease progresses is due to the progressive loss of neuronal function in different areas of the brain.

Causes

The exact cause of Alzheimer's is still under investigation, but we know that abnormal protein accumulation is key to the onset and progression of the disease.

Healthy neurons transport nutrients through microtubules that run from the cell body of the neuron all the way through to the axon. Normally, a specific protein called tau latches on to these microtubules to make them more stable, but, in Alzheimer's disease, tau detaches from the microtubules, clumps together, and gets tangled up. This then blocks the microtubules so that the neurons' transport system is hindered.

Although the microglial cells are there to help remove this unwanted tau, they cannot get rid of all the tau that is detaching from the microtubules. The glial cells recognise that they are overwhelmed and let off an inflammatory response to let the brain know that they are in trouble. This then causes inflammation in the brain, causing more damage to the neurons.

Proteins, in general, fold into certain shapes so they can perform their functions. In Alzheimer's, a specific protein in the neuron called amyloid beta folds incorrectly and therefore cannot be used by the neuron. Because it is not being used, the amyloid beta builds up to form plaques on the neuron.

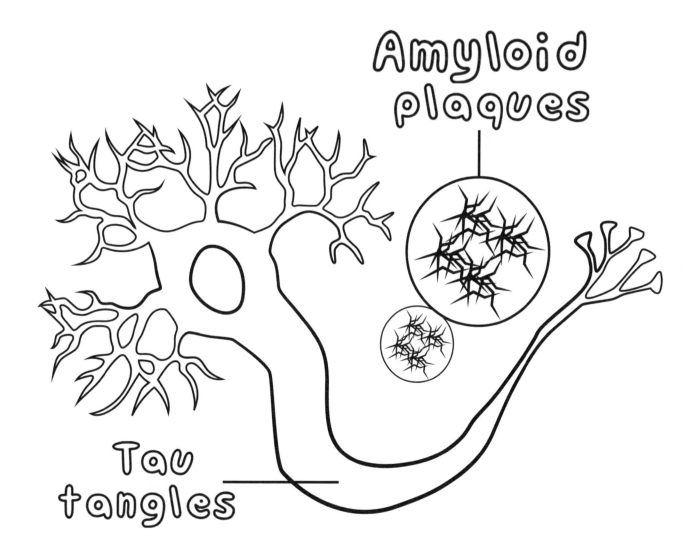

Amyloid plaques

Tau tangles

The brain struggles to get rid of these plaques, and they end up blocking arteries in the brain. This results in reduced blood flow in the brain, which can cause a breakdown of the blood–brain barrier.

Once the blood–brain barrier is impaired, glucose, which is needed for cell metabolism, struggles to enter the brain. The brain then realises that it is struggling to produce energy and lets out another inflammatory response.

Research also suggests that, in Alzheimer's patients, there is too much of the neurotransmitter glutamate, which can promote cell death.

Treatment

There is currently no treatment that can cure Alzheimer's disease, but there are medications that can slow down its progression.

A specific medication called acetylcholinesterase is used to help the neurons communicate.

There are also medications that aim to lower the levels of glutamate in the brain (glutamate antagonists).

Schizophrenia

Schizophrenia is a psychiatric condition that is characterised by issues with thoughts, emotions, and behaviour. Individuals may experience issues with their perception of reality, inappropriate behaviour, withdrawal from society, delusions, and hallucinations.

There are various hypotheses regarding the cause of schizophrenia – one of the most prominent being the dopamine hypothesis. This theory states that the symptoms of schizophrenia are due to having excess dopamine in the brain. Dopamine is a neurotransmitter which plays many different roles; the following figure shows how it is distributed throughout the brain. As you can see, dopamine is found in many different areas of the brain – and all of these brain areas are responsible for carrying out different functions. Therefore, this can help to explain why there is such a vast range of symptoms of schizophrenia (see next page).

When people think of schizophrenia, they usually have an image of someone experiencing hallucinations, as this is usually what is portrayed in the media, such as in movies. While this is correct, there are many other important symptoms of schizophrenia that are not highlighted as much.

There are many different types of schizophrenia. They are categorised based on the types of symptoms that individuals display:

- Paranoid schizophrenia: intense hallucinations and delusions;
- Catatonic schizophrenia: unreactive to stimuli, excessive negative symptoms (see Symptoms), make odd movements, lack of communication;
- Disorganised schizophrenia: disorganised speech and behaviour, illogical thinking, lack of appropriate social norms;
- Residual schizophrenia: found in individuals who have had schizophrenia in the past, but still have lingering negative symptoms;
- Undifferentiated schizophrenia: describes individuals who do not fit any specific type of schizophrenia but do still exhibit some of the symptoms.

Symptoms

The symptoms of schizophrenia are vast but can be generalised into two categories: positive and negative symptoms:

- Positive symptoms: hallucinations, delusions, illogical behaviour, hyperactivity, disorganised speech, rigid movements;
- Negative: lack of empathy, fatigue, withdrawal from society, lack of motivation, lack of facial expressions, appearing 'flat'.

It is worth noting that there are also different types of delusions, such as delusions of persecution – that is, somebody or something is out to 'get them' – and delusions of grandiosity – that is, an individual believes that they are much better than they are, such as 'godlike' or 'untouchable'.

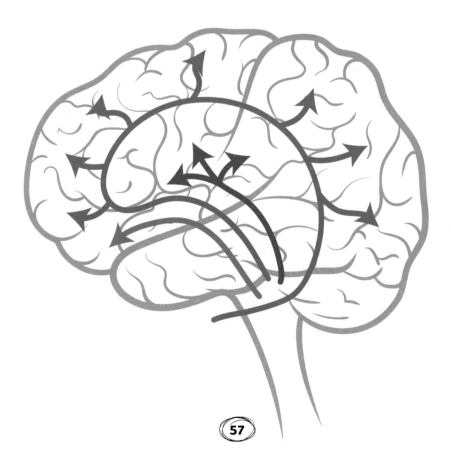

Treatments

The main treatment for schizophrenia is medication – antipsychotics being the most common. Medical professionals try to give patients the lowest dose possible – as the medication can have some adverse side effects – but a high enough dosage for there to be therapeutic benefits.

Sufferers may also be given other types of medication to treat additional symptoms, such as anti-anxiety medication and antidepressants.

The main job of antipsychotic medication is to block dopamine within the brain. It does this by blocking the receptors on postsynaptic neurons, so that the dopamine message cannot be passed on to the next neuron.

There are different types of antipsychotics that are used to treat schizophrenia, separated into first-generation and second-generation antipsychotics:

- First-generation antipsychotics block dopamine.
- Second-generation antipsychotics block both serotonin and dopamine.

The clinician will decide on which antipsychotic is best, based on the symptoms, their severity, and how well the individual reacts to the medication.

Depression

Depression is a common mental disorder. Globally, 5 per cent of adults suffer from this disorder. It can be defined as long-lasting feelings of intense sadness, lack of interest in activities the individual used to find enjoyable, and a general lack of interest in enjoyable activities.

You may often see the cause of depression being described as a 'chemical imbalance' in the brain. While this is partly true, researchers suggest that it might be much more complex than that.

Symptoms

The symptoms of depression can differ from person to person, but there are a few symptoms that doctors, psychologists, and psychiatrists use to diagnose this disorder. These include persistent sadness, anxiety, feeling 'empty', lack of interest in activities that you used to enjoy, fatigue, irritability, frustration, restlessness, pessimism, and hopelessness.

Causes

Researchers believe that there is a combination of factors that could explain the onset of depression. There could be environmental, genetic, or biological explanations. For example, people may experience depression during and after very stressful life events.

However, there are some biological and structural differences that researchers have observed in people with depression.

For example, a smaller hippocampus has been observed in those with depression. Research suggests that the more relapses of depression an individual has, the smaller the hippocampus tends to be. Research also suggests that this hippocampus shrinkage can be due to a rise in stress levels and, therefore, a rise in cortisol levels (see our stress page for more on this).

But, if the hippocampus is shrinking because of the depression, can it really explain the onset of depression? In other words, is it the depression that is making the hippocampus shrink, or are people with a smaller hippocampus susceptible to depression?

It is definitely an interesting research question – one that has not been completely answered yet.

At this point, we know that the hippocampus is involved in emotional processing and anxiety and, therefore, may play an important role in depression.

We have also seen that amygdala activity is increased in the brains of people with depression. This structure is particularly involved in processing anger, frustration, and sorrow. Increased activity in this area can explain feelings of irritability in those with depression.

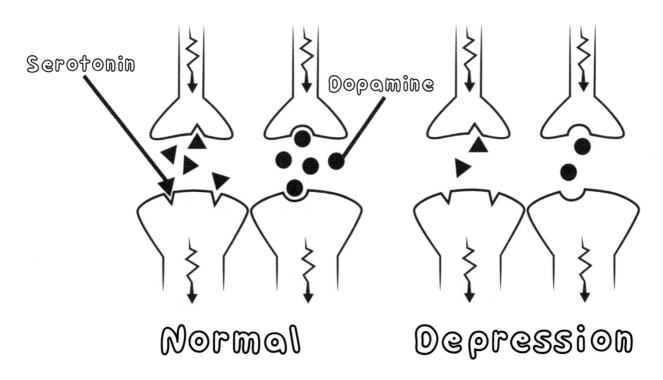

Serotonin · Dopamine

Normal · Depression

We know that the basal ganglia is an important midbrain structure that is involved in thinking, feeling, and emotional processing. Some individuals with depression have a smaller basal ganglia, suggesting that this area is less active.

A lot of research has been done looking into neurotransmitter-level differences in people with depression and those without depression. Researchers have found that those with depression may have lower levels of serotonin, norepinephrine, and dopamine in the brain.

- Serotonin plays an important role in mood regulation, sleep, and digestion.
- Norepinephrine is involved in arousal, cognition function, and stress reactions.
- Dopamine is involved in the feelings of reward, pleasure, and satisfaction.

Treatment

Talking therapies are a possible treatment for people with depression, where they can talk about their feelings and find ways to overcome the symptoms.

Another possibility for treatment is antidepressants – types of drug that serve a variety of functions in the brain.

Certain antidepressants are designed to help kickstart the growth of neurons in the hippocampus, since this is an area of the brain that is underactive in individuals with depression.

Some antidepressants can help strengthen the connections between neurons so that messages of pleasure can be sent more effectively throughout the brain.

Anxiety

We all feel nervous from time to time – whether it is before a big sports match, a first date, or a job interview or when you're going to sit an exam.

You may feel your heart beating faster, feel your body temperature rise, your palms may become sweaty. This is because your body is in its fight/flight mode. Your nervous system is working hard to make sure you're ready for action – even if there is not actual physical danger.

Of course, it's normal to feel nervous sometimes. Anxiety is when these feelings are intense and last for a long period of time. People with anxiety struggle to control these feelings of unease and worry. It can affect their daily lives and is the most common disorder.

Symptoms

There are lots of different types of anxiety, but they can be categorised into four general groups:

- Generalised anxiety: you don't feel anxious about a specific situation or issue; people with generalised anxiety feel anxious most days;
- Panic disorder: regularly feeling a sense of panic or fear; this can include panic attacks, where the body goes into an intense state of panic that can bring about mental and physical symptoms;
- Specific phobias: a strong, long-lasting fear of a specific object or situation; the fear response tends to be much greater than the actual risk of harm;
- Social anxiety: intense fear of social situations.

Anxiety is more than feeling nervous. In all of these specific anxiety disorders, people may feel sick, have an increased heart rate, blush, sweat, feel low self-esteem, have panic attacks, and have issues concentrating, along with many other symptoms.

Causes

Anxiety can be explained by both environmental factors and biological factors in the body. For example, an individual may develop a specific phobia of dogs because they have had bad experiences in the past, such as being bitten.

However, researchers have identified some biological factors that could explain anxiety.

We know that the limbic system is the emotional regulatory system in our brains. It includes the hippocampus, amygdala, hypothalamus, and thalamus. Researchers have found that there could be heightened activity in the limbic system of individuals who have anxiety.

So, this means that there is increased activity in the 'emotional' parts of the brain. For example, the amygdala is responsible for emotional processing, particularly the 'fear' response. If the amygdala is overactive, this fear response may also be overactive, explaining the intense, long-term feelings of fear and anxiety.

Scientists have also found that overactivity of certain neurotransmitters may play a role in anxiety. One particular neurotransmitter, called serotonin, is of particular importance. It plays a role in mood regulation, happiness, sleep, learning, and memory.

Research suggests that people with anxiety may experience low levels of serotonin, which may explain their anxiety and other associated symptoms.

Scientists seem to think that low serotonin could be due to:

- The body not producing enough serotonin;
- The body not effectively using serotonin – that is, the serotonin is not binding to receptors properly during neurotransmission.

Treatment

There are various treatments available for people with anxiety, including talking therapies where they can talk about their anxiety and develop strategies to combat it.

Most medication for anxiety focuses on increasing levels of serotonin in the brain. Medication that simply increases the levels of serotonin includes the triptan family of drugs. We know that it is possible that it may not be simply that there is a lack of serotonin, but that the serotonin is not being used effectively in the brain.

So some medications, called serotonin reuptake inhibitors, are designed to increase the binding of serotonin to the postsynaptic neuron. The drugs work by stopping the reuptake of serotonin in the presynaptic neuron. This means that more serotonin will be floating around in the synaptic space, so that there is more chance for the serotonin to bind to receptors on the postsynaptic neuron. This means that the neurons can now 'use' the serotonin more effectively.

Normal　　　Anxiety

Serotonin

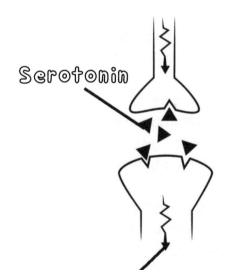

Electrical signal

Not enough serotonin

No electrical signal

Motor Neurone Disease

Motor neurone disease (MND) occurs when the brain's neurons that control motor movements (motor neurons) become faulty. The most common type is called amyotrophic lateral sclerosis.

Symptoms

Symptoms include issues with movement such as gripping, walking, and fine motor movements. As the disease progresses, patients can struggle to speak, swallow, and even breathe.

There are different types of onset of the disease.

Some patients may first notice that there is something wrong when they struggle to move their arms and legs (limb onset). Some patients may start off with issues with speaking and swallowing (bulbar onset). Respiratory onset is when patients notice that there is something wrong when they begin to have trouble breathing.

The disease is known to get progressively worse over time.

Causes

The exact reason why the motor neurons become faulty is still unknown. But researchers seem to think that specific cells (such as T-cells – a type of immune cell) in the brain are attacking the myelin and axons of the motor neurons.

Researchers have found that there are abnormal clumps of proteins in the motor neurons (specifically, a protein called TDT-43). Such proteins are responsible for controlling the genetic content of the motor neurons in their cell bodies. These clumps of proteins stop the motor neurons from being able to send messages throughout the brain and body.

We know that the dendrites, cell bodies, and axons of neurons communicate with each other through transport systems within the neuron. In MND, it appears that toxins are interfering with these transport systems. Some researchers have seen that the toxins that are usually disposed of by glial cells are remaining in the neurons, which is damaging them and stopping them from working properly.

Other research proposes that the mitochondria of the motor neurons are faulty. We know that the mitochondria are in the cell body of neurons and help supply the rest of the neurons with the energy they need to pass on messages. If the mitochondrion of the neuron is faulty, the cell doesn't have enough energy to pass on these motor messages.

Treatment

Because we don't know exactly why the motor neurons are becoming faulty, it is difficult to know how to treat this disease. Currently, there is no cure for MND, but patients are given medication to help with the symptoms.

We call these disease modifying therapies because they are not actually treating the cause of MND but are, rather, modifying the symptoms and progression of the disease.

A certain drug called Alemtuzumab is designed to stop immune cells that are potentially damaging neurons from even entering your brain. This is designed to slow down the degeneration of neurons as there will be fewer immune cells in the brain to attack the motor neurons.

There are lots of other drugs designed to do a similar thing – that is, reduce the amount of immune cells, as these are the cells that are attacking the motor neurons. Choosing the right drug will be dependent on the severity of the disease, the type of onset that the patient had, and the side effects that they experience.

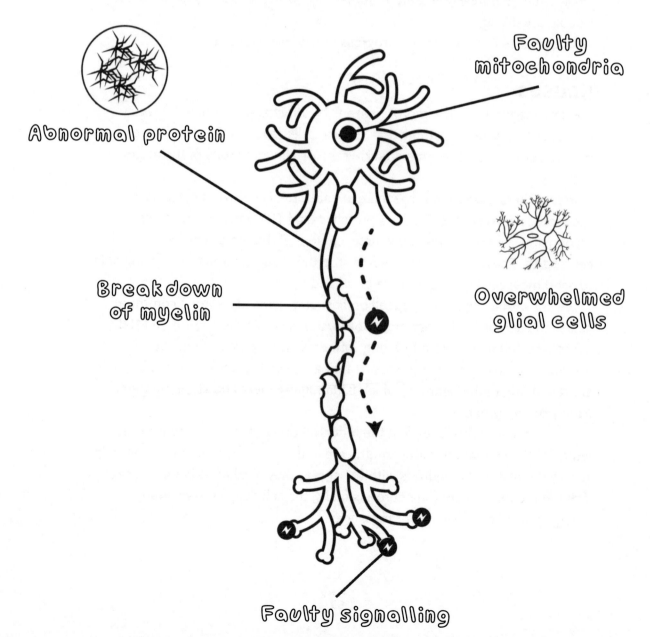

Multiple Sclerosis

Multiple sclerosis (MS) is the commonest neurological disease and is caused by an abnormal immune response in the brain. This abnormal immune response can happen anywhere in the brain. This means that there can be a wide variety of symptoms, as different brain regions are affected in different patients.

Symptoms

Symptoms include problems with thinking and learning, fatigue, bladder and bowel issues, muscle pain, weakness, mobility problems, fatigue, and vision problems.

Causes

Scientists believe that MS is caused by an immune attack on myelin. Myelin is the fatty substance that coats axons and helps speed up neuronal transmission.

So, cells in the brain that usually help clear pathogens, such as glial cells, mistake myelin for a 'dangerous' substance in the brain and try and attack it.

When these immune cells make their attack on myelin, it creates scar tissue around the axon. This scar tissue then consolidates to form plaques in the neuron.

These plaques can form in any part of the brain and they can vary in size. They hinder neuronal communication and metabolism of the neuron.

Other Potential Causes

Some scientists believe that issues with the blood–brain barrier could explain the onset of MS. If the blood–brain barrier is faulty, the brain is exposed to the body's immune response cells. These immune cells can then flood into the brain and begin attacking myelin.

Some research suggests that MS is linked to a particular virus called Epstein-Barr virus. Most people contract this virus, usually in childhood. But, just like any virus, each individual produces their own immune reaction to get rid of the virus. Scientists believe that it may not be the virus itself that plays a role in developing MS, but rather a type of immune response to the virus. This means that you can still have the Epstein-Barr virus and not develop MS. However, another individual could have the exact same virus, but their body will produce a different immune response which may leave them susceptible to getting MS.

Treatment

As we believe that MS is caused by an immune response, it makes sense that current treatment involves drugs that alter the immune system.

Patients are prescribed corticosteroids, which help suppress the immune system. It appears that, in MS, the patient's immune system is overactive, as it is attacking things in the brain that are not actually dangerous.

Another treatment option is a type of drug called beta interferon, which helps regulate the immune cells – that is, it helps the immune cells better distinguish what is 'dangerous' and what is not.

Glatiramer acetate is another treatment option that targets the immune system. It helps the body rebalance the number of immune cells so that there will be fewer cells attacking the myelin.

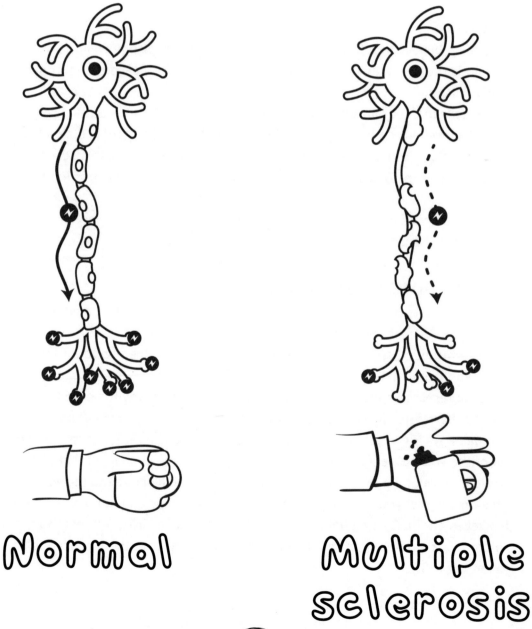

Normal   Multiple
                                    sclerosis

Chapter 7
Drugs and Medication

Recreational Drugs

So, we know that neurons are responsible for sending messages in the brain and we know that they work together with their neurotransmitters to help their communication.

We have covered how certain neurotransmitters are more prominent in certain brain areas, and that different neurotransmitters can carry out different functions. When neurons are continuously being activated by the same neurotransmitter, they create different 'pathways' or 'neural circuits' in the brain.

For example, dopamine is a neurotransmitter that is involved in reward (among many other things). Neurons that are continuously activated by dopamine messengers create a neural pathway called the dopaminergic pathway. This means that the dopamine can easily reach the brain areas that it frequently goes to. As dopamine is associated with reward, the dopaminergic pathway is also known as the reward pathway – when this is activated, it can make us feel happy and even, sometimes, euphoric.

The basal ganglia is a particularly important structure within this reward pathway. It is involved in pleasure and is a vital part of the reward circuit. Recreational drugs make this structure overactive, creating higher levels of neurotransmitters such as dopamine.

These neurons and pathways can become activated by things we do in our day-to-day lives such as eating, exercise, and sex.

However, substances such as recreational drugs can activate and increase the function of certain neurotransmitters, which produces the feeling of being 'high'.

Drugs such as cocaine can also prevent the presynaptic neuron from reuptaking the neurotransmitters that are left in the synaptic space. This means that extra neurotransmitters are floating around in the synaptic space, giving them more opportunity to dock on to the postsynaptic neuron receptors.

But a problem occurs when our brains get too used to these 'highs'. The brain becomes accustomed to these high levels of dopamine, meaning that the more frequently you consume recreational drugs, the more you will need to feel the same 'high' next time. This is known as tolerance.

Normal activities such as eating, exercise, and sex bring us pleasure. But, when the brain has experienced such highs from recreational drugs, the 'happy' feeling we get from these normal activities will feel dampened. The brain will be seeking more dopamine because it wants to activate the reward pathways. Because the brain knows that recreational drugs can create this high, it will seek to use them again in the future. This is a vicious cycle that can also explain notions of addiction.

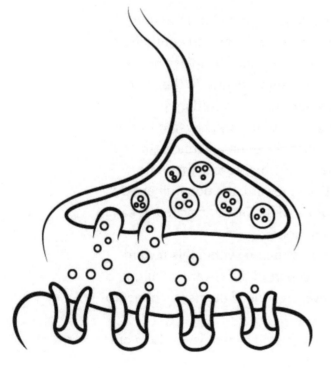

Normal neurotransmission

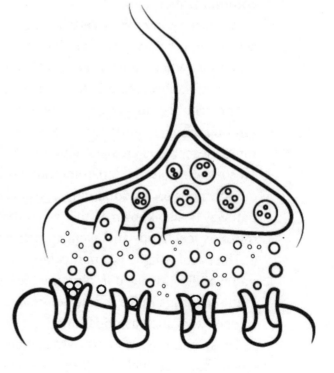

Neurotransmission after cocaine

Medication

So, we have covered how natural neurotransmission takes place. The presynaptic neuron releases neurotransmitters into the synaptic space, following action potential signals from the dendrites, cell body, and axon. Receptors on the postsynaptic neuron then snatch up these neurotransmitters in order for them to pass on the messages to nearby neurons.

We have also talked about how, for some neurological disorders, drugs are specifically designed to either increase or decrease the levels of neurotransmitters.

But how does this happen?

For example, we have talked about how schizophrenia is associated with too much dopamine in some areas of the brain. The medications for schizophrenia focus on decreasing the level of dopamine for therapeutic benefits.

When a drug is trying to decrease levels of a certain neurotransmitter, it needs to trick the postsynaptic neurons into not passing on the message in their usual fashion. Drugs that do this are called antagonists.

When someone takes an antagonist drug, the drug will be floating around in the synaptic space in the targeted brain area. When the presynaptic neuron releases the neurotransmitter, the synaptic space will consist of the neurotransmitter and molecules from the drug. The drug molecules are designed in a specific way so that they can slot into the receptors on the postsynaptic neuron.

So, the neurotransmitters and the drug molecules have to fight for their space on the postsynaptic neuron receptors. Some neurotransmitters will dock on to the receptors, but some drug molecules will manage to steal the spaces.

As we know, when a neurotransmitter docks on to the receptor of a postsynaptic neuron, the chemical message is passed on. However, when an antagonist drug molecule docks on to the postsynaptic receptor, it is not able to send the same chemical message as the neurotransmitter.

This hinders neuronal communication because the neurotransmitters cannot pass on their messages as effectively. For areas of the brain where there are too many neurotransmitters, such as in schizophrenic patients, this can have therapeutic benefits.

In some cases, however, there is not enough of a certain neurotransmitter. In this case, you would need an agonist drug.

An agonist drug molecule is able to disguise itself as a neurotransmitter. So, when the drug molecule binds to a postsynaptic neuron's receptors, the neuron will believe that it is the authentic neurotransmitter and will pass on the chemical message.

Certain agonist drugs can also help the postsynaptic receptors suck in more of the natural neurotransmitter. The agonist drug can dock on to the receptor and act like a magnet to attract more neurotransmitters to the receptor. This means that a stronger message can be sent to other neurons, as the communication due to the neurotransmitter has become stronger.

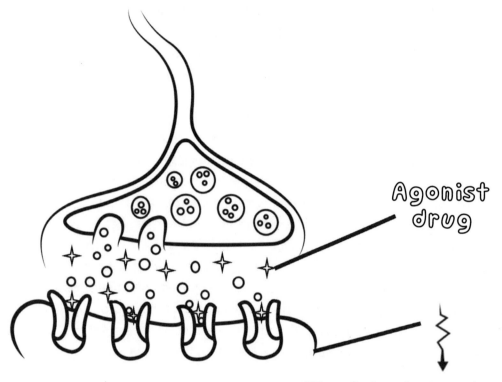

Agonist
drug

Electrical signal is passed on

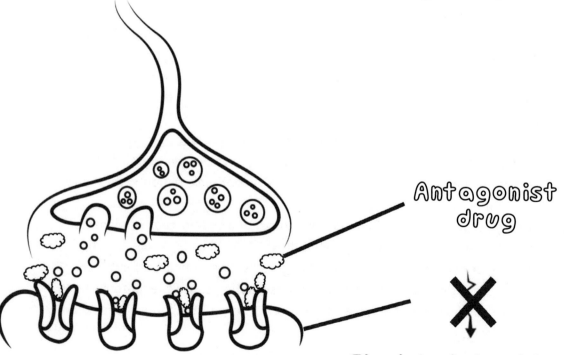

Antagonist
drug

Electrical signal is not
passed on

Chapter 8
Viewing the Brain

Brain Imaging

Before advancements in technology, the only way that scientists could really *see* the brain was by dissecting one. They did not have all of the fancy brain scanners that we have now.

As science and technology have advanced, we are not only able to view the brain in immense detail, but we also have techniques that allow us to see how the brain is functioning.

Each of the brain scanning techniques has its own benefits, and clinicians will decide what type of brain scanner they will use based on the patient's condition and, ultimately, what they are trying to see in the brain.

We will go through a few different types of brain scans and how they can be used.

Computerised Tomography

CT (or CAT) scans use X-rays to view the brains tissues and structures. A normal X-ray gives you a 2D image, but CT scans enable 3D images of brain structures using computerised technology.

Uses include localisation of tumours, viewing brain structures, looking for damage to brain structures, and looking for excess blood/fluid on the brain.

Magnetic Resonance Imaging/ Functional Magnetic Resonance Imaging

In magnetic resonance imaging/functional magnetic resonance imaging (MRI/ fMRI), there is a strong magnet inside the brain scanner that moves around the head. The magnetic field forces cells in the body to align with the magnet. A radio-wave frequency then becomes active in the scanner. The cells then go back to their normal position. Comparison of the cells' alignment with the magnet and their 'normal' position is what creates the image.

These scans can work out the levels of blood flow in different areas of the brain by comparing the MRI signal and the body's blood flow rate.

In lots of experiments, you will see that researchers ask participants to complete different tasks while in the MRI scanner. For example, they will ask them to read out specific sentences or recall events from their childhood.

This is because they will be looking at the changes in blood flow in different areas of the brain when completing the task versus when resting. As blood supplies oxygen and nutrients to neurons, researchers assume that the increase in blood flow is proportional to the level of activity within the neurons in specific brain areas.

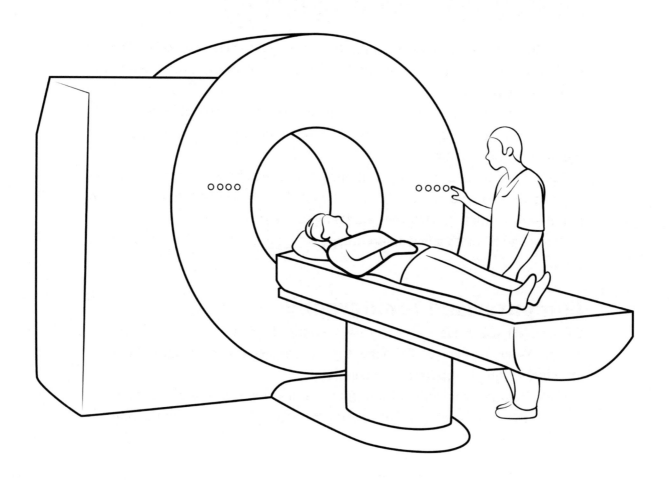

Looking at this metabolic activity in the brain areas over time (e.g. when completing a task versus when resting) is known as fMRI.

fMRI involves looking at structures and activity levels; MRI only looks at the structure.

PET Scan

We have previously covered how changes in activity in brain areas can change their structure. For example, people who experience anxiety over a long period of time may have an enlarged amygdala owing to overactivity of the neurons.

So, biochemical changes (i.e. overactivity or underactivity of neurons) usually come before the structural changes.

PET scans are used to detect these biochemical changes that could eventually lead to structural changes.

We know that neurons use glucose for their metabolism. Before going into a PET scanner, patients are injected with something called a radionuclide. This radionuclide will latch on to glucose in the body and acts as a marker to identify where the glucose is going in the brain. This indicates the activity levels in different parts of the brain.

When the radionuclide is attached to glucose in the brain, and the neurons begin using the glucose for metabolism, annihilation protons are emitted in the brain. The PET scanner can detect these annihilation protons.

A PET scanner shows the metabolism rates in different areas of the brain.

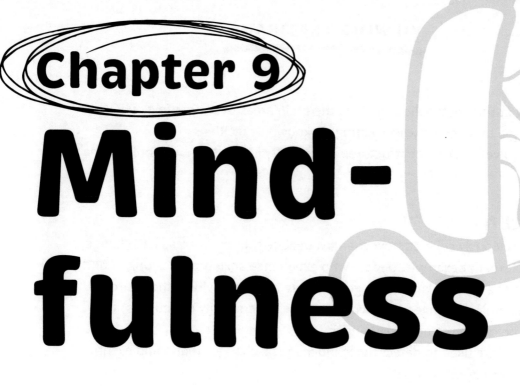

Chapter 9
Mind-fulness

Mindfulness

I'm sure we can all agree that life can be a little stressful sometimes. We've covered how stress can have damaging effects on your mind and body, making you feel tired and restless, and can hinder your concentration.

So, it's important to find ways to combat this stress, so you can focus on tasks, sleep well, and have a sense of calm throughout your day.

Mindfulness definition: the quality or state of being conscious or aware of something.

Mindfulness can also be described as taking the time to focus on one thing, letting go of all of the other thoughts that are whirling around your head.

We are all different; some people find going for a run relaxing, some people find reading relaxing, and some people find walking their dog relaxing. All of these things can bring an individual into a state of mindfulness.

There is compelling research to show that colouring can bring about a state of mindfulness. Choosing your colours, focusing on the image you are colouring, fine motor movements for each stroke of the pen – all of this brings you into the current moment and helps you focus on the task.

Research has found that mindful colouring can help improve your learning, memory, stress response, and attention and decrease anxiety levels. It can also improve your sleep and give you a sense of pride when the image is complete.

Research also shows that even 5 minutes of colouring are equal to 1 hour of meditation.

When you have exams looming, deadlines to meet, and revision to be done, it is sometimes a challenge to find the time for mindfulness practice.

So, this book is designed with all of this in mind: bringing the student into the current moment and letting them focus on one topic at a time and listen to the audio podcast while practising the mindful art of colouring. All this is designed in a way to help you learn and to leave your stress behind when you open this book.

Remember, when you are in a state of stress, your brain's energy is being allocated to the areas that govern your fight/flight response. Your body and brain think that they are in danger!

By being calm during your study periods, you are allowing the brain's energy to build new neural connections, which will aid your learning and memory.

If you take anything from this book, remember that learning brain anatomy does not need to be tiresome and boring. By breaking down each subject, understanding the topics in their simple form, and trying different learning techniques, you will reach your goal of understanding brain anatomy.

Glossary

Acetylcholinesterase A medication that can aid the communication of neurons in the brain, commonly used in Alzheimer's disease

Action potential A sequence of changes in voltage across the membrane of the neuron

Adenosine A neurotransmitter in the brain that plays a role in our sleep cycle

Adrenal glands Structures situated at the top of the kidneys that produce hormones for various physiological functions

Adrenaline A hormone secreted by the adrenal glands that is released to provide the body with energy

Adrenocorticotrophin hormone A hormone that is release in the body as a result of stress

Agonist drug A drug that aims to increase levels of a certain neurotransmitter

Alemtuzumab A drug designed to prevent specific immune cells from entering the brain, a treatment commonly used in motor neurone disease

Alzheimer's disease A progressive neurodegenerative disease causing issues with memory and thinking skills

Amygdala Part of the limbic system that is involved in interpretation of threat, fear response, and memory

Amyloid plaques Abnormal clumps of misfolded amyloid proteins in spaces between neurons, commonly observed in Alzheimer's disease

Amyotrophic lateral sclerosis A type of motor neurone disease

Antagonist drug A drug that aims to decrease levels of a certain neurotransmitter

Anterior/rostral view Viewing the brain from the front

Apoptosis Programmed cell death

Arcuate fasciculus A bundle of axons that connects the frontal, temporal, and parietal lobes

Astrocyte A star-shaped glial cell that aids the reuptake of neurotransmitters on the presynaptic neuron, removes damaging substances from the brain, protects the blood–brain barrier, directs axons, repairs damaged neurons, and maintains pH in the brain

Auditory cortex Part of the temporal lobe that is responsible for the detection of sound and the processing of auditory stimuli

Autonomic nervous system A part of the nervous system that controls involuntary bodily functions

Axon The long tail coming out of the cell body of the neuron, responsible for carrying the electrical impulses needed for neuronal communication

Axon terminal The end of the axon from which neurotransmitters are released

Basal ganglia A part of the limbic system that is involved in motor control

Beta interferon A medication used to treat multiple sclerosis that helps regulate the immune cells in the brain

Blood–brain barrier A membrane between the blood circulating in the body and the blood circulating in the brain

Brain atrophy The loss of neurons and their connections

Broca's area A part of the frontal lobe that is involved in production of speech

Carbidopa A medication that is paired with levodopa when treating Parkinson's disease to make sure that levodopa is not broken down by the body before it reaches the brain

Cell body/soma Part of the neuron that contains the nucleus, proteins, and specialised organelles such as the endoplasmic reticulum, ribosomes, and the Golgi body, all of which are encapsulated in a protective membrane

Cell differentiation The process by which cells change certain properties so that they can become more specialised and perform specific functions

Cell migration When a single cell, or group of cells, moves to different brain areas as a response to chemical signals

Central sulcus A sulcus that separates the frontal and parietal lobes

Cerebrospinal fluid The clear, watery substance that coats the brain and spinal cord

Circadian rhythm The internal 24-hour clock in the brain that regulates the sleep–wake cycle by responding to light changes in the environment

Claustrum Part of the brain that is thought to be involved in consciousness

Cochlea A spiral-shaped structure in the ear that plays a role in auditory transduction

Computerised tomography (CT/CAT) A type of scan that uses X-rays to view the brain tissue and structure in 3D form

GLOSSARY

Conscious awareness A subtype of the term 'consciousness' that includes thought processes and understanding the environment

Conscious wakefulness A subtype of the term 'consciousness' that involves basic reflexes such as sucking, swallowing, and opening the eyes

Corpus callosum Part of the limbic system that connects the two brain hemispheres and is involved in movement, vision, and memory

Corticotrophin A hormone that is released in the body as a result of stress

Cortisol A hormone that is released in the body as a result of stress

Declarative memory Memory of specific facts

Dendrites The spikey structures that protrude out of the cell body of the neuron and are responsible for receiving information from other neurons

Depolarisation/repolarisation The process of the neuron returning to its resting state following an action potential

Dopamine A neurotransmitter in the brain that plays a role in memory, movement, attention, and mood

Dopaminergic pathway Specific routes within the brain that dopamine usually travels along

Dorsal/superior view Viewing the brain from the top (bird's eye view)

Ectoderm The outermost layer of the embryo

Endoplasmic reticulum An organelle found in the cell body of a neuron and responsible for creating proteins needed for neurotransmitter release

Endothelial cells Cells that line all blood vessels

Epstein-Barr virus A common virus that can cause a specific reaction in some that is associated with multiple sclerosis

Fight/flight The instinctive response to threat where you either fight the threat or run away from it

Frequency map The way in which the auditory cortex is organised, with different parts being activated and responsible for the processing of different sounds based on their frequency

Frontal plane A vertical plane running from side to side, dividing the brain into anterior and posterior sections

Functional magnetic resonance imaging (fMRI) A type of scan that uses magnetic fields and calculations of blood flow in various brain regions to determine brain activity in different parts of the brain while different tasks are completed

Ganglion cells Cells in the retina of the eye that send signals regarding visual information to the optic nerve

Gestation The period of developing in the womb between conception and birth

Glatiramer acetate A medication used to treat multiple sclerosis that helps balance the number of immune cells in the brain

Glial cells Cells found in the central and peripheral nervous system that are responsible for providing support to neurons and maintaining a healthy environment for the brain

Golgi body An organelle found in the cell body of a neuron that processes the proteins made by the endoplasmic reticulum and sorts them ready for transportation; it also plays a role in controlling substances coming in and out of the neuron

Grooves Folds/bumps on the cortex giving rise to the 'pattern' seen on the cortex

Gustatory cortex Part of the frontal lobe that is responsible for perception of taste and flavour

Gyrus (plural gyri) A ridge/small fold on the cortex giving rise to the 'pattern' seen on the cortex

Haemorrhagic stroke A stroke resulting from a burst artery in the brain

Hippocampus Part of the limbic system involved in learning, memory, and spatial navigation

Homeostasis The constant self-regulating processes in the brain that ensure the correct conditions for survival

Homunculus/little man An image of a man showing the areas of the body that are most sensitive to touch and, therefore, occupy more space on the somatosensory cortex

Hypothalamus Part of the limbic system that helps regulate hormones, mood, sex drive, the sleep–wake cycle, and hunger

Interhemispheric fissure A fissure separating the two hemispheres of the brain

Ischaemic stroke A stroke resulting from a blocked artery in the brain

Lateral fissure A fissure separating the frontal, parietal, and temporal lobes of the brain

Lateral geniculate nucleus Part of the thalamus that plays a role in the relaying of visual information

Lateral plane A horizontal plane running through the middle of the brain, from left to right in a lateral view of the brain (like cutting a burger bun!)

Lateral view A view of the brain from the side

Levodopa A precursor for dopamine in the brain, commonly used in Parkinson's medication with the aim of increasing dopamine levels in the brain

Long-term memory Memories that we can retrieve from that past at any moment

Lunate gyrus A gyrus in the occipital lobe

Macrophage A type of immune cell that helps remove pathogens

Magnetic resonance imaging/MRI A type of scan that uses magnetic fields and calculations of blood flow in various brain regions to determine brain activity in different parts of the brain

Medial frontal gyrus A gyrus situated on the medial part of the frontal lobe

Medial temporal lobe Part of the temporal lobe that is involved in memory

Medulla oblongata/myelencephalon Lowest part of the brain stem

Melatonin A hormone that is produced in the brain in response to darkness and regulates the internal circadian rhythm

Meninges The three layers of the cortex

Microglial cell A type of glial cell that helps remove any damaging substances in the brain and redundant synapses, monitors activity of synapses, and aids growth of dendrites

Microtubules The structural backbones of axons and dendrites that allow chemical messages and nutrients to be passed along the neuron

Midbrain/mesencephalon Topmost part of the brain stem

Mindfulness The quality or state of being conscious or aware of something

Mitochondria An organelle found in the cell body of a neuron that helps the neuron have energy through metabolism

Motor cortex Part of the frontal lobe that is involved in planning and controlling movement

Motor neurone disease A progressive disease causing issues with movements such as gripping, walking, and fine motor movements; it can eventually affect speaking, swallowing, and breathing

Motor neurons Neurons that are responsible for relaying information regarding movement to and from the brain

Multiple sclerosis A neurological disease caused by abnormal immune responses in the brain, resulting in problems with thinking, learning, mobility, and vision

Myelin A fatty substance that wraps around the axon of the neuron to help speed up neuronal communication

Myelination The process of myelin formation along the axon of the neuron

Neural plate The thickened plate of the ectoderm of an embryo that gives rise to the neural tube

Neural tube A tube that is formed following the folding of the neural plate and later becomes the brain and spinal cord

Neurogenesis The growth and development of the brain, neurons, and nervous tissue

Neuron A cell that is responsible for relaying information from the body to the brain (and vice versa)

Neurotransmitter A chemical substance that is released from neurons in order to communicate with other surrounding neurons

Neurulation The folding motion (morphogenetic phases) that transforms the neural plate into the neural tube

Nodes of Ranvier The small gaps situated along the axon of a neuron

Norepinephrine A neurotransmitter in the brain that regulates arousal, attention, cognition, and stress response

Odorant receptors Receptors found on sensory neurons in the nasal cavity that are activated when specific odours are detected

Olfactory bulb A structure in the forebrain that receives neural input regarding odours that are detected via odorant receptors

Olfactory cortex Part of the frontal lobe that is responsible for the processing of odours

Oligodendrocyte A type of glial cell that helps create myelin and provides metabolic support

Optic nerve A collection of millions of nerve fibres that sends information regarding visual stimuli to the brain

Papillae Bumps on the tongue that contain taste buds

Parasympathetic nervous system A nervous system responsible for calming the body down and conserving energy

Parkinson's disease A progressive neurodegenerative disease that causes issues with movement as a result of degeneration of dopamine neurons in the basal ganglia

Pathogen A bacterium, virus, or microorganism that can cause infection or disease

PET scan A type of scan that uses a radionuclide to observe metabolism rates in different areas of the brain

Pineal gland A gland in the middle of the brain responsible for endocrine function

Pituitary gland Part of the limbic system that regulates growth, metabolism, reproduction, stress response, and lactation

Pons (metencephalon) Part of the brain stem that links the medulla oblongata to the thalamus

Postcentral gyrus A gyrus in the parietal lobe of the brain where the somatosensory cortex is located

Postcentral sulcus A sulcus in the parietal lobe that separates the postcentral gyrus from the rest of the parietal lobe

Postsynaptic neuron The neuron that receives the neurotransmitter during synaptic transmission

Posterior cortex The 'sensory' part of the brain

Posterior parietal cortex Part of the parietal lobe that is involved in spatial navigation and eye movements

Posterior/caudal view A view of the brain from the back

Precentral gyrus A gyrus that makes up the somatomotor cortex

Precentral sulcus A sulcus that lies parallel to the front of the central sulcus

Premotor cortex Part of the frontal lobe that prepares the body for movement and is involved in co-ordination of limbs

Presynaptic neuron The neuron that releases the neurotransmitter during synaptic transmission

Primary motor cortex Part of the frontal lobe that is involved in complex movements, specifically voluntary movements

Ribosome An organelle found in the cell body of a neuron that uses genetic information to create proteins

Sagittal plane A vertical plane that goes from front to back, diving the brain into left and right hemispheres

Satellite oligodendrocyte A specific type of oligodendrocyte that regulates fluid levels within the brain and helps repair myelin on the axons of neurons

Schizophrenia A psychiatric condition affecting a person's thoughts, emotions, and behaviour

Sensory memory A type of memory that consists of things we may have quickly acknowledged but not specifically remembered

Sensory neurons Neurons that are responsible for relaying information regarding the senses and environment to and from the brain

Serotonin A neurotransmitter in the brain that regulates mood and attention

Serotonin reuptake inhibitors A collection of drugs that increase the binding of serotonin to the postsynaptic neuron during synaptic transmission

Short-term memory A type of memory that allows us to remember information that we need in that specific moment but will later forget

Somatosensory cortex Part of the parietal lobe that receives all sensory information from different parts of the body

Stem cells Cells with the potential to develop into different types of cells

Stroke Medical emergency where oxygen supply to the brain is hindered, causing death of neurons and damage to areas of the brain

Substantia nigra Part of the limbic system involved in the production of dopamine, movement, learning, mood regulation, and judgement-making

Sulcus (plural sulci) A groove on the surface of the brain

Superior colliculus Part of the midbrain that controls our bodily movements in response to visual stimuli

Superior frontal gyrus A gyrus situated on the superior part of the frontal lobe

Sympathetic nervous system The nervous system that governs the fight/flight response

Synaptic cleft/synaptic space The space between the presynaptic neuron and the postsynaptic neuron

Synaptic pruning The removal of synapses that are unused

Synaptic transmission The communication between two neurons across the synaptic space

Synaptogenesis The formation of synapses in the brain

T-cell An immune cell that helps fight off pathogens and protect the brain from disease or damage

Tau tangles Abnormal clumps of tau proteins in the neuron, commonly observed in Alzheimer's disease

TDT-43 A protein that is responsible for controlling the genetic content of motor neurons; abnormal clumps of this protein are associated with motor neurone disease

Thalamus Part of the limbic system involved in pain recognition, memory, the sleep–wake cycle, and relaying sensory information from the nervous system to the cortex

Transient ischaemic attack/mini-stroke Medical emergency where oxygen supply to a specific brain region is depleted for a short amount of time

Transporter proteins Proteins that help transfer substances across the membranes of other cells

Triptan drugs A collection of drugs commonly used to treat anxiety disorders that increase levels of serotonin in the brain

Ventral/inferior view View of the brain from below

Visual cortex Part of the occipital lobe that processes visual information

Wernicke's area A part of the left temporal lobe that is involved in comprehension of speech

Index